MW01123630

BEST POETS OF 2015

VOL. 4

John T. Eber Sr.

MANAGING EDITOR

A publication of

Eber & Wein Publishing

Pennsylvania

Best Poets of 2015: Vol. 4
Copyright © 2015 by Eber & Wein Publishing as a compilation.

Rights to individual poems reside with the artist themselves. This collection of poetry contains works submitted to the publisher by individual authors who confirm that the work is their original creation. Based upon the author's confirmations and to that of the Publisher's actual knowledge, these poems were written by the listed poets. Eber & Wein, Inc. does not guarantee or assume responsibility for verifying the authorship of each work.

The views expressed within certain poems contained in this anthology do not necessarily reflect the views of the editors or staff of Eber & Wein Publishing.

All rights reserved under the International and Pan-American copyright conventions. No part of this book may be reproduced, stored in a retrieval system, or transmitted in any form, electronic, mechanical, or by other means, without written permission of the publisher. Address all inquires to Rachel Eber, 50 E. High St., New Freedom, PA 17349.

Library of Congress
Cataloging in Publication Data

ISBN 978-1-60880-490-0

Proudly manufactured in the United States of America by

Eber & Wein Publishing
Pennsylvania

A Note from the Editor . . .

Throughout the year I receive letters from today's poetic traditionalists who find it unfitting that we publish and recognize poems that do not rhyme; to many, rhyme is an essential component of a poem. These letters always draw a smile, as they remind me fondly of similar scoldings I would receive by my grandmother for using my debit card for online purchases, for permitting my son to watch Spongebob Squarepants rather than something more "appropriate" like Looney Tunes or Tom & Jerry, or for using the GPS on my cell phone when a map will get me anywhere I want to go. I would simply smile . . . and keep my rebuttal to myself. Where poetry is concerned, however, I must respectfully disagree with the arguments made in these endearing, handwritten notes that ever so gently admonish us for publishing poems and selecting winning poems that are written without end rhyme.

The truth is non-rhyming poetry, or *free verse*, not only *exists* but is alive and validated more today than ever. I hold no grudge, however, toward these voiced disputes. As a matter of fact, I have utmost respect for those poets who seek to uphold and respect the timeless, old-world style of poetry consisting of rhythm, rhyme, and meter; to write a poem in this form and write it well—free of forced rhyme, unsteady meter, and inconsistent line lengths—is not easy to do. I do, however, attempt to enlighten these poets by mentioning one name—Walt Whitman, the American modernist poet who fathered the free form style and brought about a revolution of sorts to 19th-century literary society and academia. His famous collection *Leaves of Grass*, which boldly deviates from standard rules of meter and rhyme and acceptable language and motifs, caused quite a controversy during its sporadic appearances and various editions in the mid to late 19th century. Today, however, this iconic collection—once scorned for its arbitrariness—is used all over the world as a teaching tool in the literary arts.

Since the time of Whitman, many have followed in his footsteps with this chosen style: Ezra Pound, Emily Dickinson, Wallace Stevens, D. H. Lawrence, T. S. Eliot, William Carlos Williams, Billy Collins, and former US Poet Laureates Robert Pinsky, Natasha Trethewey, and Juan Felipe Herrera just to name a few. Herrera was named US Poet Laureate in June 2015 and is the first Chicano to ever receive this honor. In comparing Herrera's work to Whitman's, James H. Billington, representing the Library of Congress, calls Herrera an "American original"; similarly to Whitman's *Leaves of Grass*, Herrera's poems "engage in a serious sense of play—in language and in image—that I feel gives them enduring power . . . I see how they champion voices, traditions and histories, as well as a cultural perspective, which is a vital part of our larger American identity."

The underscoring of the American identity in their works can only be carried out through free verse. Linear freedom of the free form style is what inspires the poetic voice to speak freely and encourages unrestrained thought. For both Whitman and Herrera, their lyrics are "freeing"—freeing of attitude, beliefs, emotions, opinions, observations, and judgements. To have all of these notions confined to a set rhythm and line length would not only produce a poem that is completely ineffective but wholly untrue. The meaning would be buried in syllables and feet, with the poem's overall purpose still begging to be released from within the poet's soul. In 1855, Whitman simply took the American credence of freedom and ran with it. Today, poets like Herrera not only carry on the American tradition of free verse style but have taken it to new, successful levels, proving further that poetic artistry can be just as pleasing to the mind as it once was to the ears and eyes.

At the very least, I hope I have persuaded many of you, formalists or not, to get to know the work of these prolific authors and become further acquainted with this contemporary, non-confining style of writing. Perhaps attempting this style will even encourage you to broaden your repertoire of themes. Don't be afraid to push yourself in surprising new directions!

Rachel Mueck
Executive Editor

The Road

On the road
Down the road
Fork in the road
Middle of the road
Bump in the road
Rough road
One for the road

Road rage
Road to something
Road to success
Road to nowhere

Take the high road
Look before you cross the road
Don't go down the wrong road
Take the road less travelled

Road toward freedom

To be idle is a short road to death
The road not taken, take the long way or take the short cut
The road to hell is paved with good intentions
Go with the flow or it's a hard road to hoe
I want the highway (now here's a different road, fast, fast, fast)
Hit the road Jack and don't you come back no more

No wonder it's easy to get lost in life, so many roads!

Jennifer Rice
Lacey, WA

Prudent Practice

When words are many, attractive by desire,
prudent thoughts often fall aside.
Foolish needs, greed enriched, become the path.
Hope then turns worldly, for riches of the earth.
Pride and arrogance.
Dark paths driven.
Prudence seeks to uncover sin. Be silent, still, listening for Him.
Your heart senses unrest,
sweetness of the lips speaks simple.
Beware of paths that lead to death.
The Lord takes pleasure in those who fear Him,
In those who hope in His mercy, Psalm 147:11.

Tim Moyer
Spokane Valley, WA

Discarding My Shiny Blacks

Years laid wasted, in desperation of parental approval.
Forever ending… in satisfying the impossible.
I truly ponder, as where to begin.
Then I suppose, it was in the very first breath of…
"It's a girl!"
Not on me, nor your dying breath of stubbornness.
From recollection,
I gave it my unwavering all, to become…"Daddy's Girl."
But with over a half century past, finally the message is lucid.
I'm wiping away my tears.
I struggle, dispelling the imaginary lump from within my throat.
My broken fantasies fading in the distance…
Like… the somber church bells on Sunday.
No disrespect intended…
I'm kicking off my dulled, shiny blacks; hoping they hit you…
Like… your '62, "Runaway Train," Jimmy "B"!
Seek your final absolution, as I lay upon your cheek a single kiss.
Silent, my words evade me…
I void your legacy of ebony misery, blowing dust from my memories.
No longer shackled to your worldly burdens, I rise from my sorrows.
Kicking from my feet, the tiny, shiny, dulled, black, shoes…
I can no longer bear the constraint.
I pray, for my desire to forgive you…
Therefore, healing a soul, unwanted…
Goodbye Daddy… (ox)

Lauri J. Gerace
Fabius, NY

Miracles

Miracles can be a special sign,
Miracles of God's power you will find!
Miracles of love you want to see,
Miracles of life are in you and me!

Miracles can come from up above,
Miracles can be like two turtledoves!
Miracles can be found in me and you,
Miracles know just what they can do!

Miracles can be found in people you know,
Miracles come but they can always go!
At a wedding you will find Jesus turned water into wine!
Look in the Bible because it's there all the time!

Miracles can have a beautiful loving glow,
Look and see what miracles can show!
Miracles can come from all around,
Miracles of *wonder* can always be found!

Miracles can be found in the holy Bible or a book,
Miracles are something beautiful that need a look!
Miracles can be found on a pretty day,
Miracles will always seem to want to stay!

Miracles are a part of your life,
Miracles are something you need to look twice!
Miracles can always play their part,
Miracles will always be in our hearts!

Carol Gough
Collinsville, MS

I have been working for a long time and I love what I do! I like writing, reading and creating new poems. I also love reading poems from other authors. There are many hobbies I like to do. What inspired me to write my poem is that you see miracles every day and it's wonderful!

Long Ago

Long ago I opened my eyes
and blinked to golden light.
Before there was darkness.

I no longer float in liquid,
but out to breathe my new air,
to move in my new world.
It was long ago.

But I still remember.
I close my eyes now.
I leave in darkness.
The golden light is going out.
I am floating away,
being as I once was free,
long ago.

Mike Tobin
Sun Valley, NV

The Decision

Your life has been a circus
Since the day that you were born
Some days have all been sunshine
Other days a vicious storm
Some days you were so happy
Other days you seemed so sad
But you always seemed to manage
'Cause the good outweighed the bad

When you think of fame and fortune
As you crawl in bed at night
You grab your old brown teddy bear
'Cause you got to squeeze him tight
You dreamed you went to Heaven
Danced with angels all night long
Then you woke up in the morning
And those angels were all gone

As you continue down life's pathway
All the roads you choose to take
You'll find the answers to your questions
In the decisions that you make

Samuel Bennett
Sturgis, SD

Compliments

You look so fine in that new dress
Head turns! You'll have no lack.
Oh, this old thing I've had for years?
The style is almost back.

Your speech was so informative
The things you said were right.
It took no time to get it done.
I wrote it in one night.

Your poems are so true to life.
They'll surely pass the test.
I hope the judge thinks just like you
They're not my very best.

You are so cultured in your ways
People look up to you
They don't get very close at all
Like entries in Who's Who.

You give a friend a compliment
A negative they find.
It's almost like they do not know
Success and peace of mind.

Now that you know that's what you do
Please pause and think it through.
When kind words come into your view
My friend, just say, "Thank you."

Lloyd Broomes
Tuscaloosa, AL

I've been featured by Poetry.com, International Who's Who in Poetry, and now Eber & Wein Publishing! Although this invitation is quite an honor, I hesitated. For several weeks I procrastinated. Then as the deadline approached it happened. An unplanned international phone call connected me with a family member, and we chatted briefly. Switching to Facebook to continue our regular conversations my sister commented that I was cultured, causing me to become victim of the ubiquitous habit of downplaying compliments. She protested, "Just say thanks." My impoverished upbringing triggered something in me, and in that moment her comments planted the seeds for this poem.

That Old Blue Chair

In my living room is a blue recliner
Of all my chairs there is no finer
It was handed down to me
From my loving family

Each morning with my coffee cup
I sit and sip 'til I wake up
My aches and pains just melt away
Until I'm good for another day

Yet I'll linger there and dream a bit
Of long ago, when I was fit
Of things I did and didn't do
Some make me smile, some make me blue

Nevertheless I spend much time
In that comfy chair of mine
Spending many an hour in prayer
Giving God my every care

It brings such comfort everyday
It's really hard to break away
But one thing sure you know is true
I'll always love that chair of blue

Virginia Henry
Dunellen, NJ

The Key

When I look out at this world,
I feel like I'm in a box,
And pray I find the key that fits the lock.
The struggles here feel like a test.
Does one know the answer better than the rest?
Through stress and fear I breathe a sigh,
If I answer wrong will I die?
Then I notice the cover has a vent,
And I do believe it was heaven-sent.
A light shines through from above,
It's bright and warm and filled with love.
Then I realize I've found the key
That will open this box and set me free.

Teresa Clanton
Kingston, TN

Grade Book

The trouble is you cannot know or take account
of struggle. All you know is what came out,
not what went in or what went on inside.

And all those days I wrung my rafters bare
while they sat, slouched in desks, or picked
their nose and smeared it in a book. After class
I scraped my words from off uncaring walls
and glued them back inside my skull, there
to hang like hooded bats till I, their keeper,
call them forth to flap their wings
in other sleeping skulls.

                          But something
had to happen! In fifteen weeks a carrot
sends out healthy roots, but even a cactus
cannot root in wooden chairs. Yes,
*some*thing — if only how to land that lovely
blonde across the room, or what their catcher
should have called the time their weakest hitter
cracked a hanging curve across the fence.

And while I suspect that's the most of it,
I still contend that grades in a book
can't measure minds. At any rate,
I'm still too busy measuring mine.

Joseph H. Kempf
Indianapolis, IN

Life of Regret

She called, he had to go
    right from the start
Why didn't I listen to
    the gnawing in my heart

As the days turned into years
    his behavior didn't change
Somehow I had decided
    to endure this constant pain

She had a spouse, as did he
    his love for me
continued for her
    our love was not to be

As I reflect on my life
    through all the ups and downs
I wonder why I lost myself
    as I am still his wife

Judith M. McKillip
Iowa City, IA

SRO

Walk the West side, no rest
The last straight show to the test
Playing shy to the East side beasts
Debtors hiding as debts increase

Marble spiral stairs, don't they look the best
Deceptive fantasy to confide what's next
Some such mirage granted last not least
Undisguised reside yourself as guest

The guide toward the highest jewel, the view
Never mind the pests
The reflective ceiling is no more
Your head
Your bed
Is on the floor

Share cold water, as well as deathly chores
Do as they say or be kicked out the door
No money is enough
To be above the level poor

Susannah Mellett
New York, NY

Unsettled

Change, the mere word scares me, the thought of it
frightens me, its actuality petrifies me.
Lately, I am overtaken by a seemingly insurmountable
mountain of it.
Spinning uncontrollably around in a whirlpool's rotation.
Its mighty force tugging me downward against my will,
robbing me of the contentment I wish to maintain.
My comfort zone bombarded from all sides.
Combating them is a challenge. I must adapt and find
strength, difficult for the weak, yet I try tirelessly so.
Some changes I knew in time I would greet. Those faced
somewhat easily as days pass, others brutally gut punch me.
I want to curl up in a ball to suppress the hurt.
Longing for courage to get by each, in time, on my own.
To reach the summit, tame the raging waters, and
barricade the blows of change.

Barbara A. Mahoney
St. Mary's, PA

A Beautiful Place with Many Lodges

A golden eagle circles high above,

A beautiful place where there are many lodges for an eternity
Which our native brothers know our creator dwells eternally
In a realm of purest love in a place of sanctity and inviolability
Colors so deep it fills this place with an unique personality
A rainbow forms an arc above the lodges in common solidarity
Transcending this holy place into breathtaking spirituality

Some call it Heaven, or the happy hunting grounds forever
Still others call it "The Other Side Camp," I call it the altogether
Lodges of white buffalo skins, given by the white owl's feather
Fourteen to sixteen buffalo skins shield from dangerous weather
Taken from the sacred white buffalo's purest white leather
Facing the east, eagle pins, hold the lodge together

Stakes secure it to the ground by the badger's powerful insight
A wolf guards the entrance to the lodge, keeping out blight,
A grizzly bear covers the doorway, ensuring that all is right
A coyote guards the lodge during daylight,
An owl guards the lodge during the night,
A mountain lion guards the doorway with his great might

A white dove sends down our creator's great love

Alice Marie Young-Lionshows
Lodge Grass, MT

A Place in My Head

There's a place in my head where we're treated the same
And my children never have to experience pain
The wicked are always punished for their sins
And a pair of loving arms is where life begins

There's a place in my head where everyone is safe
There is no crime, there is no hate
Nobody steals and nobody lies
There's nothing but happiness, so nobody cries

There's a place in my head where truth is always told
No one is hungry, no one is cold
Every child is cherished, not hurt or abused
No one is fake, forgotten, or used

There's a place in my head where life is joy
And everyday is like a brand new toy
We all die of old age because there is no disease
And we all are free to become what we please

There's a place in my head where every potential is met
There is no money, so there is no debt
There's a place in my head where everyone is free
If only this place didn't belong to just me

Robin N. Stradley
Oroville, CA

I'm a thirty-year-old wife and mother of two beautiful sons, ages five and one. My husband and I have been married six years and I truly believe he is my soul mate. I have been writing stories and poems since I was about four and songs since about seven. I have been published several times, but it is my dream to publish a novel or a book of poems. I am in my third year at Ashford University earning a BA in applied behavioral science to be a mental trauma counselor. This is a huge honor for me!

An Awe of Beauty in January

While gazing out of my kitchen window at the clear blue,
January sky,
my eyes caught a glimpse of the bluest blue bird flying by.
I closely watched him trying to perch upon the top of a twirling
weather vane in the cold wintry wind.
He continued flying in a circle, patiently waiting to make a land.
He suddenly flew to the very top, trying to hold on tightly with his
tiny brown feet.
His perch there was only for a moment, when he flew down onto
the brown, cold ground all covered with twigs and leaves lying
against a dark barren tree.
His body was so… blue and his breast the deepest red, he looked
as though he was wearing his bright winter vest.
He continued sitting there gazing at me, turning his bright blue
head from side to side.
With all of his posing for me, he seemed to say, "Am I not the most
handsome thing you have seen all day!"
He seemed to know he had filled my heart with such warmth and
awe on this cold wintry day.
Suddenly, his posing for me came to an end, all of his awe and
beauty was up and off flying into the cold, January wind.

Janice Nokes
Lebanon, TN

Sisters Three

Once when we were very small
Our hearts and lives were joined
By threads which loosely weave
Sisters three are we

We laugh, giggle without restraint
Dancing, singing—the threads tightened
blood and life, our souls entwined
Sisters three are we

We hug and support through highs and lows
road trips, good times wrap us close
Our hopes we shore, our dreams we cherish
Sisters three are we

Bereft are many of binding threads
blood does not a sister make
Joy, tears and secrets shared built our bonds
Sisters three are we

Virginia Diane Troxel-Spence
Loomis, CA

Mighty Redwood

Oh, mighty Redwood,
You once stood so tall,
Oh, mighty Redwood,
How, great was thy fall,
Oh, mighty Redwood,
Tales of your escapades spread far and wide,
Oh, mighty Redwood,
It's hard to believe they were all just lies,
Oh, mighty Redwood,
You once stood among the best,
Oh, mighty Redwood,
Now you're nothing more than a shriveled up, decaying pile of flesh,
Oh, mighty Redwood,
You were once revered and respected among the trees,
Oh, mighty Redwood,
Look at you now, lying dead among the leaves

Tera Levette Wiseman
Houston, TX

Princess

Our first family dog
We had an outstanding fourteen
years together wish we could
have had more time with
you so dainty, and calm peaceful
and happy we will miss
you greatly always and forever
I hope you are at peace
now running through doggie
heaven

Victoria Drost
West Springfield, MA

Birthdays

Birthdays come but once a year
Rejoice and do not fear
The unknown of getting older
Just live life more bolder
Live each day as if it is the last
Live for the future… not the past
Birthdays are to be celebrated
Show the world you are elated
To live another year
Shouting… I am here, I am here!

J. Lillie Townsend
Orrum, NC

For My True Wife

If love exists, it exists with us,
If love is known, mine is known for you,
If love was ever true, it is yours for me,
Since love is real, ours is forever thus.

When day begins, it starts for us,
As light continues, so love is full.
Your shade is near; your mist is here,
Your love rings like the Angelus.

And as our days creep by and pass
We love for today; we love for what we are.
And when that vast tomorrow comes
I know that love is eternal, it continues,
It lasts.

Leonard Blessing
New Providence, NJ

Leonard Blessing has been writing poetry all of his life. Some are love poems as is this one. Others are about nature and friendship and some are of world conditions. He has read his poems at reading sessions to very good applause. He started his career working for the Prudential Insurance Company and after four WWII military years he went to college and became a science teacher at Millburn High School in New Jersey. He had been an athlete and had an amazing career helping coach the high school team to seven conference and two state championships.

Untitled

My darlings,
Take me to church
Provided we attend my funeral.

These, the best years of our lives?
Why stick around,
Waiting for them to bottom out,
To get monotonous.
Why live at all if not foolhardy.

The next time you see me in these four walls,
It'll be for my funeral.
You all will mourn for me.
Don't be sad, now
Talk.

Keep me alive with words;
Remember my drive,
My adventure,
Turn me into a legend.
A bedtime story, if you will.

That is immortality, my darlings.

Beth Shiller
Youngstown, OH

Today I'm Wearing My Pearls

I'm getting ready to go out, no work for me today!
So adorned am I, with all of my clothes, and makeup,
I've only one final touch. My pearls, I'll wear my pearls today!

There's a story behind these lovely gems from the sea.
An oyster in agony made his own nacre to form them
Just for me.

My lovely pearls are made from layers and layers of nacre,
That made each one colorful, shiny and smooth, of much value
To me, and the oyster will never know of his impact,
From what is born from him, down beneath the sea.

We are like the oyster, we have our own grainy imperfect
Nature. We too are being shaped and refined into something
Priceless and beautifully unique. We don't fully comprehend
The beauty and love of God's own merciful "nacre."
His only Son's agony traded for us on a tree.
We are the pretty pearls molded from God's healing
Balm. His spiritual nacre shapes us into persons,
(Potential spirit bodies) worthy of his promised eternity
Of peace and love. We are being crafted for Heaven.

That heavenly place where we no longer struggle with life's
Woes, a place of serenity we finally find.
Pearls! Pearls! I'm wearing my pearls.
Today I'm wearing my pearls. My pearls and
"My pearls."

Diane Loretta King Hampton
Romulus, MI

A Change in Directions

I lived a life of sidewalks for a while,
All the time wearing a fake smile.

Then one day, in a storm,
I couldn't do it anymore.

I said goodbye to my love that day
And tearfully walked away.

I held my head up high,
But inside was a fearful sigh.

Each time someone would ask,
I'd say I'm fine and wear my mask.

When alone, I cried for hours each day,
Hoping and praying to find my way.

Through a few steadfast friends,
My heart started to mend.

I searched my heart on my knees
And waited for God to set me free.

I never expected the miracle He sent!
My freedom was in me to believe!

To believe that I know where I belong
And with the angels I can't go wrong.

Now my path is shaded by trees,
And my walkway covered with leaves.

The wind blows my hair,
And away goes my cares.

Because I took the time
To listen to this heart of mine.

Peggy J. Kash
Ocoee, FL

Two Hearts

When two hearts meet a wondrous thing
Enlightens their lives, the world just sings
A love enhanced with a mystery from above
That is unexplained, but must be love
A love that seeps deep into their hearts
A love that no one else can share
A love eternal, that will last forever
A love that two hearts implore

Yes, when two hearts meet, a miracle then doth begin
A journey only they can share
From year to year
A life of happiness, joy, giving, fulfilment, peace
A life to explore, a life eventful,
A life to strive, a life to gain, a life of contentment
Forevermore
When two hearts meet

Colleen N. Frankland
Kariong, NSW

Class Reunion

Do you remember when…
    we studied side by side,
Classmates, friends, competitors,
    how the years did glide!

Do you remember who…
    was walking by your side
As you hurried to your classes,
    neath our principal's watchful eye?

Do you remember who…
    was cheering at the games,
Who danced with you on prom night,
    or won in sporting fame?

Teachers strictly guided us,
    they strived to help set goals,
We graduated "Class of '47,"
    just 50 years ago!

In my kaleidoscope of memories,
    I see your smiling face,
Your hand raised high up to the sky,
    the alma mater plays!

We're all so glad you came today,
    to help us celebrate,
Our special anniversary, and
    to set another anniversary date!

Marjorie Hamm
Wisconsin Rapids, WI

Fare Thee Well Love

Strolling along the hills of green,
Vivid wildflowers beside the stream.
Trees are lush and fragrance fair,
The breeze is gentle, warm and rare.
My mind wanders to memories of you,
The laughter we shared, the heartaches too.
Just five short years but so much love,
Then you returned to the spirit world above.
Seniors Homes challenges can be difficult at best,
Your room easy to find, you were seldom at rest.
With a smile on your face you welcomed me,
I'd sit by your side your face I could see.
Your life you shared, not an easy start,
A Scottish orphan rejected, hard to play your part.
You married, had children, did well along your way,
You offered love and humor every single day.
You helped me through trying days, we laughed hard it's true,
We were good for each other and hopefully I helped you.
We shared so much laughter left memories on my heart,
It gives me strength to endure now we are apart.
You left me for the spirit world at age of eighty-nine,
My heart broke, I still talk to you wonderful friend of mine.
I shall be eternally grateful to have you as my friend,
We'll meet again in spirit when my journey comes to end.

Helen Margaret Spears
Guelph, ON

I met Jean in the retirement home where I work. We just instantly clicked and had the most wonderful relationship of laughter and good times… We also had times of tears and support as her health declined. She was so excited that I am going to Scotland on my tour next year for my sixty-fifth birthday. This was written with great love, respect and thanks for the wonderful memories, Catherine Jean Hollings… *I shall look back on all the fun we had together when my days are heavy and difficult, and I shall remain* grateful…

Beautiful

From the moment of first eye contact your beauty overwhelmed
me, struck a note deep inside me!
At times I wonder why you?
Then I look into those eyes and those eyes smile and look back at
me, no more reason to question, no more doubt!
You're the one I've been waiting for!
A true friend, someone to look forward to seeing that maybe just
maybe is feeling the same way inside as me.
The love in those eyes makes my heart skip a beat, knowing yet
not that this might truly be a friendship made for all eternity!
Your eyes like hands caress me, hold me captive!
The touch of those eyes sends a message of adventure and
anticipated happiness that I have been looking for in so many
wrong places.
Possessed by those eyes and the beauty that lies for the moment
hidden within, threaten to overwhelm me, consume me, yet, at the
same time create this new me!
With a somewhat reckless abandon I run headlong to thee.
Overwhelmed by the strangeness that you have created with just
that way you have of looking at me.
With friendship and kindness that is not a sham or a fake, the
genuineness of someone who is very real, loving and with a
gentle kindness.
So thank you much for coming into my life!
At a moment when I think we both need this much needed
affection and the attraction that is like the glue that binds us.
A wonderful way to start any day!
This looking at you with your way of looking and smiling back at
me, can only be described or expressed adequately (seems to me)
by saying —
"Beautiful,"
A word so fully expressed in and by you!

Joseph P. Demicco
Channelview, TX

Colors

Colors of the rainbow are almost
always in my view

The ocean and the sky
different shades of blue

White, beige, pink in the sand
so soft, but you can hold it
in your hand

Birds, black, grey and white
always in the sky
but not at night

Shirley Harmison
Daytona Beach Shores, FL

Love

You don't love someone for their looks or fancy car or their money.
You love them because they can sing a song only your heart can
understand and you can pray and go to church with them. One
you love, love is nothing, to love is something to love and be loved
is everything.

Marie Green
Inverness, FL

God's Anointing

God's anointing, what is it? I was sent
to try to give you the answer and then I
will quit. The anointing of God is not
free and that is the first thing that
you must see. God's anointing you can
feel and by his anointing you can get
healed. When the anointing of God
comes up on you there is so much power
there until you don't know what to do.
It will make you move, laugh and cry
truth and not a lie. God and his anointing
will make you feel like you can fly.
God's anointing to explain it to you I am
doing my very best to try. It is God's power
alone and right now it is hard for the
to leave this word alone. So I am going
to finish it and get gone. God's anointing
is a gift to the body of Christ to me that is
amazing and very nice. It is given to God's
saints for a divine reason and this poem
is being now written for this time and season.
People of the world it is God's anointing that is
on me to be able to write this word to thee.
God gave his anointing to set all men free can you see?

Earline Hagwood
Columbus, OH

My name is Earline Hagwood. I write poetry as I receive inspiration from God's spirit to do so. It is a gift like the anointing that God has allowed me to use to be a blessing to the world and anyone that will read this poem. I would like to thank God, my heavenly Father, for this gift because the Bible says all good and perfect gifts come from above to my heavenly Father. I honor you and I love you always.

The Human Loss

Death leaves an emptiness in one's heart, which no one can replace. It has taken the human spirit to an unknown place.

Whilst we journey here in this land, may we enjoy the moment of this precious and priceless gift of life.

Let us learn to resist that which does not edifies, but that which brings forth the good Spirit from our being unto all whom we touch, sending forth Divine peace, wisdom, and beauty, to the Temple of the inner man, unto all those who accept it.

Our mortal life here on earth is so short, so we should try to make our experiences fruitful and dynamic, and not cause pain for ourselves nor others.

As situations of life afflict our mortal being mentally, spiritually, physically and, at times we are subject to disease, and sometimes procrastination that affects our life. Therefore, while we travel towards the final end and, as our journey comes to a closure:

May we go peacefully and dignified, onto the next pathway of life.

Beverley Ashman Cunningham
Kirkland, QC

Meant to Be

Sometimes we, as writers you see,
Tell the greatest of lies to ourselves
Sometimes we, as humans we be
We run, and we battle, as well

Sometimes we, as oppressors we are,
We turn a blind eye to the land
Sometimes we, as animals at heart,
We spit and we snarl and make a stand

And sometimes I, as shallow as I am,
I see the world as so much more
But sometimes I, with my heart in my hand,
Sit and listen to the legends and lore

For are we not all, in some shape or form,
Exactly what we were meant to be?
Are we not all, through the sun and the storm,
So blind, and yet, all of us see?

Sydney Chilson
Junction City, KS

What Is in a Name?

Before one names a child he should know the meaning of the name, when given it are we actually the definition of our name? Or do we stray from the meaning because we become opposite of the name? Or is it that we do not care what was bestowed upon us to claim? For ages people have rated themselves as they wish, not what they gained, if we truly are the person we were born will we stand and reign? Have we learned that morals, principles, honor, chivalry, obedience, patience, peace and humility are not a game? Are we enough human to serve and care for other mankind until the end of time? Yet, a name is not just a definition but, what you do with it to gain your fame, would you rather be one of the lust, power, greed, that brings shame? Or would you rather be one who defies fear to fight the odds gaining a priceless gift that tames? Not one who seeks revenge by killing with bitterness, hate without shame, what kind of people are we today or are we living in yesterday's game? Have we learned nothing by the defeat of the seekers of greed, lust and fame? Will we make our world a circle going back in ancient times and minds, are we hearing the laughter of our ancestors seeing this civilized world far behind its time? Because we refuse to pay attention to our own fate of what's yours and mine? So what does the future hold for us or are we blind? Will our graves be a place of rest or simply a place to pour the lime? Keeping away disease hoping to stop it from killing us this time, maybe new are the disease if we refuse to see the signs of the time, I ask you what then should we do to present disaster to shine? Or are our eyes, ears, mind, floating in circles as the water in the mind? Life is precious, sacred and priceless where money is only a sound, ringing in our ears chiming as blows the rhymes, will we awake to save ourselves before it's too late to dine? Or will we starve and choke ourselves over the ages of time? That name you will give you the answer if you listen to its chimes.

Martha Finley Foreman
Kearns, UT

I am writing this poem because of the situation our society is in at the moment. For centuries people have labeled each other by their nationalities, gender, and color of skin, but mostly because of their last names. It has been said the last name defines us most definitely as well as our first names. In some ways, I tend to agree, but do you want your child to have a strong name that will and others as well as not? How carefully are you picking your child's name and do you know what it means especially for the future? What about the children who will be named after this person? Have you given that child something to live for and to look forward to? Will you bring peace and harmony into the lives of the numbers of your family or reason and killing as was done in ancient times for greed, lust, money and power? The question is yours to answer, do you know what to say: I will make my family proud or I will shame my family by the wrong I bring into this world?

The Backyard Gardener

Blest are those who work the earth
Plant their seeds in early spring
Enjoy fresh radishes, in twenty-five days
See God's creation, and you wonder
How could anyone, not have faith

Blest are those who work the earth
Feeling that pride in their efforts
Eating good food, without pesticide
And having that peace of mind to meditate
In the splendor, of the sun and fresh air

Then there are times, to lay down the hoe
Reflect on the beauty, that's been sown
Feel that labor of joy and relax
Stop worrying about those pesty old bugs
Give thanks, to the summer sunset and harvest

Blest are those who work the earth
Like any good friend or neighbor
Whose garden wisdom and humble faith
In their own backyard of glory
Sometimes, grows those big — red — potatoes

Donald D. Dunlap Sr.
Greensburg, PA

Untitled

Before I die I want to hold you, kiss you like I never held and
    kissed you before.
Before I die I want to make love to you like I never made love to
    you before.
Before I die I hope we get lost in love and nobody will be able to
    find us.
We are here today and gone tomorrow.
We got to love each other like we never loved each other before.
Love is the key to all things, any kind of problem that you go
    through together.
Love is the key to open the door to happiness, joy, heartache and
    pain that we go through.
I just want to love you women like you have never been loved before.
I want to touch you and feel you.
I want to kiss you all over and over again.
I don't want to stop loving you.
I want to love you, love you forever, until I die.
I want to give you a part of me and you give me a part of you.
I want to hold on, hold on so tight to you until there is no tornado
    or hurricane that can tear us apart.
Oh, women I just want to love you, love you like it's no tomorrow.
I want a pure and clean love.

David Cook
Fort Pierce, FL

Vet Distress in the US

A dirty blanket was where she did sleep.
Her stomach was hungry for food to eat.
She'd served three tours in Afghanistan.
There she had eaten figs and lamb.
In the dumpster she found stale bread.
It was better than nothing she said.
Her worldly possessions were in a sack.
She hoisted it, carrying it on her back.
Her parents were both deceased.
A home and decent food looked bleak.
The Army had stated, "We'll care for you."
Nothing they promised had come true.
Over a year ago she had come home.
Now alleyways were where she did roam.
Every day she thought, "It'll get better."
Cold weather was here.
She had no coat or sweater.
"How much for the Silver Star?"
The pawnbroker looked at her from afar,
"Ten dollars is what I'll give."
"But, I need money to live!"
"Get a job. Stop begging me."
"Better I'd died in a foreign country.
Home in my US has no place for me."

Jeri D. Walker-Boone
Laurens, SC

My Hero... My Daddy

My hero...
Your picture is just a captured moment to smile back at me
I talk to you.
I pray with you.
If only you could touch my face.

My hero...
You are missed... please give me the strength to make it through
each day.

My hero...
From your soul to mine, together strength will conquer the fears
of tomorrow.

My hero...
When I was scared to face tomorrow... you hugged me.
There was the strength that I needed.

Growing up, the squeeze of your hand told me all will be okay.
Your wisdom... if only I listened better.
Your nurturing... allowed me to become the mom I am today.

Where did the days go? How did the years pass?
I keep your photo by me... reminds me you are still here
My hero... my daddy... forever your little girl.

Denise Hernandez
Bay Shore, NY

Acquaintances

Starburst Spacemen and Hurricane Losers
They were the teams and we weren't substance abusers
The doctors and nurses could be called accusers,
But I don't see it that way.

Your shirt said "Kahlúa"
I told you a story.
You laughed out loud.
Now guess what my dog's name is.
Just one guess.

Well, you know, I think you're cool,
But I'm the quiet kind.
Still waters sometimes overflow with emotions so deep.
A lot like Twining's tea that has to steep.

Now what do I do?
What do I say?
You'll call me one day? Well, that's not enough.
Is she really your wife—have a nice life!

Starburst Spacemen and Hurricane Losers
They were the teams and we weren't substance abusers.
The doctors and nurses could be called accusers.
I think you see it that way.

Paula Pardo
Baltimore, MD

The Crimson Chair

I enter slowly,
a spider on tiny
cat feet runs along
the wall's edge.

Shadows dance on
surfaces like ghosts
of bereaved souls.

In the corner, a
crimson chair sits
naked and alone,
still the old
hermit of solitude.

Secrets hide deep
in the folds of
this empty space,
and a god, if he is
near, exists quietly.

The spider reappears,
undaunted by me
or darkness falling.

The crimson chair in
its silence watches,
as if it were
the only guardian of
this secluded sanctuary.

Norm Keehn
Thunder Bay, ON

Secrets

My darkly twisted heart is wrenching with desire,
Of a life not yet fulfilled,
Not yet perfected.
A flutter of a breeze stirs the current embers,
Of this unmistakable yearning,
This unmistakable burning.
My dreams insist upon an existence without the hiding,
Of my true essence,
My true defense.
Now a glimpse of this future I see,
Through an obvious portrait,
An obvious gate.
Everything is now clearer than glass,
Through understanding of actions,
Understanding of creations.

April Simpson
Garland, TX

Reaching...

Sometimes I feel
from you —
all the things
you do not say.

Your hands reach out
and touch my humanity.

I reach back —
amid the broken pieces
of my life —
do my very best to make:
a bouquet for you.

Cheryl Yarek
Mississauga, ON

I have been a mental health advocate for twenty-five years. The reason I chose this path is because I was inspired by the beliefs, values, and actions of a phenomenal psychiatrist. She was my psychiatrist but a serious illness incapacitated her. I wrote "Reaching..." early in my therapy with her — as a tribute to her ability to reach and engage.

My Swan Song

Remember me, I know you do.
My clothes are too big; my eyes dull blue.
I barely smile, nor do I laugh.
I sit very still while peers walk past.

I'm the one with the ashen hair.
My dress is too long and shows of wear.
A crooked bow, a drooping sock,
Is what the children usually mock.

When we play games, I'm always last.
And when I run, I'm not that fast.
It's hard to come to school each day
When no one you know wants to play.

When I grow up, I won't always be
This ugly duckling that you see.
With passing years I'll be refined,
A lady who is well defined.

And when you pass me on the street
Will you remember when we meet,
That awkward child from days long past
Who only wanted a friend?

Deborah Grochowski
Milwaukee, WI

Dear Dad, We Love You

A letter to our dad, our angel in Heaven:
You taught us to live each day like it's our last,
To treasure everyone and everything,
To smile always, even through the hard times,
To never give up no matter what,
To be patient and kind,
That the show must go on,
That education and family is important,
That we should laugh often,
That love is best shown and spoken,
That we should be generous and serve others,
That we should always have hope,
To respect ourselves,
To believe in ourselves,
To get back up and dust ourselves off when we fall,
To have strength,
That things happen for a reason,
That we shouldn't fear the future,
That we should embrace the future,
That we should always try our best,
And that everyone is unique and special in their way.
You will always be in our thoughts and hearts.
You will always be there with us on our journeys.
We hope we are making you proud.
We love you Dad,
Always and forever!

Morgan Elizabeth Coldwell
Midland, MI

I Was Only Minding My Business!

As the leaves from the gusty wind settled on the ground rapidly,
in the streets that would forever changed my short lived life,
the air seemed quite tranquil and melancholically timorous,
with signs of wonder penetrating its face, only I could feel.
No worries or disturbing signs from the past ever crossed my ego,
as I embarked on a very dark, solitary journey all alone,
one that would make others' nerves quicken, saliva thickens
until words of solace would become as scarce as precious gold.
Past malaise have tainted the true meaning of being an American,
yet nothing that would prepare me for that horrible nighttime,
under the skies I walked; my eyes on nothing else but a little fun,
was that too much for a teenager to ever expect?
Had I known that day would be my last I'd have held onto those
I love,
and fully embraced the dear memories we'd shared,
however, someone else had plans: tactics exercised decades ago,
which now resurfaces anew in the hideous state of Florida.
If to protect and to serve was 100% factual that day,
I'd have been alive to tell you my side of this dreadful chronicle.
Sadly, I "stood on your ground," with two deadly weapons in hands:
oh yes, a "bag of skittles and a can of iced tea," vicious arsenals!
Fearful! Your gun's near, "Don't follow" ricocheted in your ear,
deep inside, that's not what you needed to hear,
too overzealous to get rid of another type, by any means necessary;
tough luck for me, Sunshine State will set you free, end of story!
What happened on February 26, 2012, was never part of my reverie,
"I was only minding my business and now I no longer exist."

Fritz-Gerald Delice
Dacula, GA

What truly stirred me to write "I Was Only Minding My Business" was the superfluous 2012 slaughter of Trayvon Martin, a black teenager in Florida. America seems to alienate itself from the fact that, in the twenty-first century, "racism" still exists and unless we acknowledge the severity of such a disease, bury the hatred that certain groups continue to hold today, as a nation, we'll remain far from obtaining God's mercy and grace. This piece serves as a vow's renewal, taken for people like Emmett Till, Stephen Lawrence, Eric Garner and Michael Brown, whose families are still asking the "why" question.

Do Not Give Me Your Tears

Do not give me your tears, for I am beyond their reach.
If you cry it is for you, and not for me.
Do not mourn me with heavy hearts and sad faces.
My joy was in your laughter and your smiles.
Where I have gone there is no place
For the sorrow of the living.
I am beyond the pain and sadness of this life.
Do not give me your tears, but give instead your smiles.
Remember me with joy, and I will stay forever
In the hearts that held me dear.
Enfold me in the sunny days of summer,
Wrap me in the scent of roses,
Bathe me in the taste of wine.
Do not give me your tears, for I am beyond their reach.

Pat Sanderson
Doncaster, S. Yorks

Oh Africa

I hear a symphony.
I hear music in the air,
Beats of a drum, being played everywhere.

Your motherland, our people are getting closer to you
Now you tell me what, what are you going to do?

Your native land our people are here,
Ready to spread love and bring about good cheer.
They've come from afar, out of this country
Trying to do the best they can and didn't
Have any money.

They've walked many miles and have no shoes
On their feet, no clothes to wear, not even
Something to eat.

Baskets on their heads, I've got to finish
These chores, running through the fields,
Y'all sure is making a whole lot of noise.

Get up at sunset, no rest at sundown,
No peace, nowhere, nowhere to be found.

Climbing hills and had to go through many
Mountains, hungry of a thirst, I've got
To drink from this fountain.

Cumbya (Cumbya) I hear you calling,
What is man to do when everything is falling?

I hear a symphony; I hear music in the air
Beats of a drum, beats of a drum, beats
Of a drum, being played everywhere.

Valerie L. White
Danville, VA

Salute to Our Soldiers

Thank you to our military heroes,
those brave men and women who serve!
They've given their all for our freedom,
past and present, full-time and Reserve!

They've given their precious lives
for our safety and freedom and rights!
They've been killed and badly injured
in many long battles and fights.

They've been away from their loved ones
for many endless nights and grueling days.
They've given their all without hesitation
in so many courageous and amazing ways!

They are all our fearless heroes —
Army, Navy, Air Force, Marine, Coast Guard and Reserve!
They are the front line of our hard earned freedom!
In the United States military we are so proud they serve!

We are the United States of America!
We will *always* stand tall and proud and strong!
Thanks to our brave military men and women
who've protected our freedom all along!

Judy M. Gregg
Florence, MS

Seasons and Trees

Seasons come and seasons go,
just like the trees—always changing.

Winter finds it cold and so
much snow—
and the trees always bare.

Spring finds the snow has
melted away—
and the buds are coming out
on the trees.

Summer finds us enjoying
the sun—and everything
in bloom: the flowers in
all the bright colors,
and the trees a great shade
of green.

Fall we get the cool breezes,
and the leaves falling to
the ground,
the crunch of leaves under our feet.

Oh the love of the changing
of the seasons and the trees
story of the leaves.

Sharon G. Rutledge
Brooklyn Park, MN

A Servant I Am!

Scripture says God will watch over our coming and going.
God, you must be tired 'cause I sure am.
Amazing how many ministries I can embrace each week,
The ones you hand me plus the others I seek.

I'm sorry to say some fizzle out; why is that God?
Each one has your name attached.
Oh, they must choose you—do they expect a miracle?
Or that an angel will drop from Heaven to sustain them?

Teach them love, God, and open their eyes and hearts.
I'll keep trying to lead.
Course I haven't perfected following yet!
Could we do it together—you and me?
Oh, that's what you intended—now that sounds splendid!

How exciting! In partnership with the Lord Almighty!

Sandi Graber
Rochelle, IL

Seasons of Life

Our life is based on seasons
we have
childhood
young adults
and
maturity
Along our life we discover and
praise our creator
for
the precious gifts he
bestows on us
and
we are content
knowing
His love is constant
and we
are His creation
and under
His
protection

Ellen J. Correa
Orlando, FL

The Dream

Once upon a time a man had a dream,
Freedom and hope were more than a gleam:
The building with the cross was a place of hope,
Freedom from racial hatred, it helped folks to cope:
The bomb blew up in the middle of the night,
It destroyed everything at the site:
Freedom and hope now paid the price,
Was this too much of a sacrifice?
Ashes were all that remained at the site,
Racial hatred won the first round in this fight:
Soon people came from everywhere,
New freedom and hope soon filled the air:
Brick by brick and board by board,
Freedom and hope were soon restored:
The building stood complete and tall,
The bell began to ring freedom's call:
The people soon finished up inside,
It was full of hope, glory and pride:
Racial hatred had lost, its head hung in disgrace,
Soon peace and love helped filled this place:
When people are united, there is great power,
This will be freedom's finest hour.

James W. Mayou
Mashpee, MA

Love Said She

"Love," said She
Sickness crawled in each vein, each cell
Bleak, dark, dank, it slithered
Leaving a blackness, a gaping hole
She called, She cried, the pain ripped through
Gasping, holding, twisting, heaving upwards
Was anyone listening? Did no one see?
Still it slithered, unhindered, a path of deadly destruction
The tears rained down, filling the rivers, the oceans
The sun baked, dry and hot
The smell of death; destruction covered the ground
The child gently picked the wounded flower,
Folded stem, head drooped, dullness oozing
"Why is it dying? What can I do?"
"Love," said She, "and all will be well"
A gentle kiss, a drop of water
Nurtured that flower to seed
Standing tall, it reached to the sky
A tree grew, becoming a forest, rich in life
Animals thrived, insects buzzed
A field of flowers blossomed
A kaleidoscope of color once more
Fed with a child's love,
Like fire, it burned the darkness away
And once more, She became, a woven tapestry
"Love," said She, "and all will be well
Does it take a child to see?"

Jackie Hardcastle
Ottawa, ON

On the Boat

Weary was an understatement
as he rested on the cushion at the stern of the ship.
Heavy eyes closed in sleep while unseen guardians
watched over the preacher, the healer, the goodness
who showered never-seen-before gifts on seekers,
faith being the only currency he accepted in return.
Deep in his slumber, a dark cloud encroached and
at first winds softly swayed the vessel, gentle cadence
rocked the master back and forth… back and forth…
but quickly gusts drove deep black waves into frenzy
that spilled over the craft, threatened to swamp it!
Squall fury drowned out the voices of seasoned sailors,
replacing years of nautical confidence with dread,
unmindful that a greater presence traveled with them.
So they cried out, *"Do you not care that we perish?!"*
Stinging rain on cheek, biting words on heart,
wearily he stood to confront this tempest.
"Peace! Be still!" And just like that, it was over.
Wind and sea and sky all bowed to his will.
But school wasn't out yet.
"Why are you afraid? Do you *still* have no faith?"
Penetrating questions for twelve men who daily
witnessed the miracles of Jesus the Nazarene…

In his care, peace can be found in the midst of storm;
I for one intend to stay on the boat very close to him.

Diana Roth
Greenville, SC

Treasures

As the colors of the rainbow
With the different shades of green
And the multitude of hours
With remembered dreams I had
You surprised me
With your friendship
And gave wings to my delight.
You are the jewel
I discovered in the treasures
Of my heart.

Elaine J. Yuzuki
Gardena, CA

I wrote my first poem at age nine. I have had no formal training. I write when the Spirit speaks to me in beautiful sayings; I put them down on paper. Poetry makes me think at a deeper level. I wish for everyone to ask herself/himself: what can I do to help my community? Right where I am with the talents I have, that is my wish.

Months of the Year

January brings a snowy cheer
February with its icy days
In March our kites we fly
April with its many showers
May to cause to bring the flowers
June to say the school goodbye
July gets so dusty and dry
For fair August, September makes
The leaves turn brown, November puts
Them safe to the ground, for Christmas
And December, because this is the month
Of our Lord and Savior's birthday
Thank you Lord for these beautiful
Months of the year

Alice M. Clark
Burlington, NC

Hold On

I know my heartbeat and the feeling that comes over me when you
  are near,
I hold you like a precious lover who fills my every need.

My face lights up when you touch me, like a shining star.
You are the knowledge which I seek.
The wisdom that you share brings confidence
And support from which you hold me up.
The mirror in which I look to see myself as the beautiful person I am.

You enhance my every step —
You take away all my fears,
Your strength excites me and your playfulness I adore,

When we walk hand in hand with love, a whole new world appears.
I see a new horizon and an intense sunset, the moon glows while
  the breeze blows in the night.

This is not a fantasy, it is a dream come true.

Jolly P. Stickley
Lynchburg, VA

*I live in Lynchburg, VA. I'm the founder of Energy Restructure Emotional Clearing.
Poetry is an expression of my true feelings. Writing brings me comfort and peace.*

Fall of Man

Feel me breathe
See me seethe
While blood flows
Into the ocean of my life
As I see the sweat drip from your pores
Who am I, if not you?
We are all the same
We are all flesh
I pull the sky from its heavenly frame
And shake the stars off
As if dusting the rug beneath my feet
Where is he?
The one that hides
Behind my breath, I can feel him
In my mind, I see him
This place of skin and bone
Is all that I have known
Lift the haze upon my eyes
Let us see all that the sky hides
Let me look into the black
And see the sunrise upon your chest

Jeffrey J. Michalowski
Singer, WI

Contentment

Are your golden years
slightly tarnished,
do they need polishing
up, just a bit?
Get involved in a good
Bible group meet, and
you will never want to quit.

Tell your friends how
you are hurting,
they may also be.
Pray together, in agreement
and Holy Spirit will
show up, you'll see.

Bless all my dear
sisters and brothers.
God made us all
one family, in Him
to love and care for
each other, and never
go out on a limb.

May God bless you all
and keep you watching,
as He promised He
will return, to
be forever with Him
in our new heavenly home.

Esther Hackett
Lewistown, PA

Dreams

Dreams express what is
in our hearts

Dreams can make us
happy and laugh

Dreams can make us
sad and cry

Dreams can help
guide us

Dreams can make us
stronger

Dreams make life
bearable

Dreams can show us
the past and future

Dreams are like hope
we need them

Irene McFadden
Conway, AR

I have had great enjoyment from writing poems. I have shared them with my family. I will leave these poems to remember me by and for the generations to come. My family and friends have encouraged me to write more.

Not the End

Five years ago this Mother's Day, my blessed mother passed away.

Death is not the end my friend, on that fact you may surely depend.

For all that are in the graves will hear God's voice: your resurrection is not a matter of choice.

"…They that have done good unto the resurrection of life. And they that have done evil, unto the resurrection of damnation." See John chapter 5, verse 29. If you want to go to Heaven, walk the narrow path line. Search the scriptures that you may find, eternal life through the Savior divine. Jesus Christ our mediator is listening for a sinner's prayer, while sitting next to his Father in the sanctuary up there. When all the pardoned ones' slates are wiped clean, the sanctuary will forever gleam. As wicked men continually reject God's grace, love and mercy, his Holy Spirit is grieved and gradually withdraws from the earth. Probation will close for the entire world. See Revelations chapter 22, verse 11. Upon that prophecy fulfillment, you will either be doomed for Hell or sealed for Heaven.

Bernice Hooks
Los Angeles, CA

This is dedicated to the righteous who have hope in this death. Jesus Christ died for the sins of all humanity to save us from eternal death by burning into ashes in hell fire. God loves the world and desires to give us the kingdom of Heaven when we believe He died for us and accept salvation by faith.

Peace of Mind

I'm looking for something that I can't seem to find
Something that's not so very different,
But an allusive kind.
It seems to get nearer when the church bell chimes
Then drifts farther away like today's sign of the times.

I just keep looking for something
Like an individual in a crowd
Then it quickly slips away like feathers
On a snowy white cloud.
I know it's just down the road on a street that is paved
Or way back in my memories
That I have very carefully saved.

Whatever it is, it's an ethereal mystery
To the likes of me.
I know it's there and it's something I really want to see.
It's surely many things and not just answers
To what I can learn.
I really want to find it,
Though I don't know which way to turn.

It must be a vision that is true for nearly everyone
And something we must achieve
Before our feeble lives are done.
It's something I'll keep looking for
And I know that I will find
That special happiness that comes with complete peace of mind.

Donald A. Thieme
Enid, OK

Not long after writing this poem, my dad passed away peacefully at the young age of ninety-two and a half—I'm sure he has now found "complete peace of mind."

To Be a Man

To be a man must be *oh* so grand,
With muscles so big and strong!
You were endowed with the strength and fortitude,
To work the whole day long!

You have the vision to see the broken part,
Of whatever work you assume.
You make planes fly, computers work,
And even reach the moon!

God gave you the strength of Sampson,
You are not afraid of a lion!
You will go to the door in the darkest of night
While I quake in a dark room!

You leave a home of luxury and comfort,
To find the end of a rainbow!
You slay a tiger and search for gold,
A man is so fearless and bold!

You sail the seas and fight a war,
To protect your woman at home.
The world is so glad you care,
But your life to often is not spared!

Doris Shields
The Colony, TX

Best Friends

A teardrop gathered in my eye
As I reminisced on why
Simple pleasures have to end
Like sharing time with an old friend.

Seeing the old elm tree brought to mind
A much, much earlier time
When we would sit beneath its shade
Laughing and chatting as our children played.

As the sun made its circuit
So would we
Moving our chairs
Around that wonderful old tree.

But things change, those days long since gone
Our children now have children of their own.
One old friend moved away
But the old elm tree still stands today.

Many times has its leaves turned from green to gold.
Those two young friends have now grown old
But naught can change the friendship they made
Just spending time in the old trees' shade.

Please God one day permit
That one more time under that old tree we may sit
Sharing our blessings without end
Especially for the years we've been best friends.

Marian W. Brattland
Prior Lake, MN

Walk On in Jesus' Name

When your days become dark
and your burdens seem to
wear you down, look up and
walk on in Jesus' name.

There are times that you may
feel depressed you think the
journey isn't worth the time,
and you just, don't want to
put the effort in it. Look
up and walk on in Jesus'
name.

When the cares of this world
come against you, nothing
you do seems to be
worth standing up for.
Family and friends turn
against you. Remember you
have to see Jesus for
yourself, look up and
walk on in Jesus' name.

Geraldine Jennings
Hampton, SC

I enjoy writing because it helps me to relax. Hopefully, I will be able to do my book of poetry. I am just glad that I can submit my poems through Eber & Wein Publishing.

People You Meet

People you meet some can be sweet,
Some can be rotten, and have a personality that can be forgotten.
People can have a sense of fun, or make slight remarks and run.
People can stab you in the back, or could cut you some slack.
People can be cheap, and also those need to take a flying leap.
People can be warm at heart, and never know when to start.
People can be high on life, and take on children and a wife.
People can be hurt in certain ways, and not make sense on other days.
People can be sick in the head, and get that way from lead.
People can do right or wrong, and still have the sense to be strong.
People have ways of getting ahead, but yet they stay around and
act dead.
People in all their glory, get together and have a different story.
People that can walk away, learn to live another day.
People who have love and care, will always be there to share.
People will be who they want to be, and not care about what you see.

Louis R. Santiago
Niagara Falls, NY

Clouds and Sunshine

White clouds drifting in the sky
    Softly, silently passing by
Suddenly, the dark clouds come rolling in
    Twisting and turning until the rains begin
Just as quickly, the bright sun bursts forth
    Oh look, there's a rainbow to the north
Clouds and sunshine all over the skies
    A gift from heaven right before our eyes

Frances Riddle
Greensburg, PA

Given to Us!

As we pour our words out, in hopes,
That someone hears, to follow those words,
And help make clear, the word of love.
To understand, just what, we are doing
Here. Focus on our actions, as focus
Becomes clear!
To realize, what we have done, in the
Face, of the one.
Showing we, as us, to become as one!
To feel what life, is really about, to us.
Not to destroy, his gift to us.

Gregory Bangs
Lake View Terrace, CA

Someday

There comes a time in our lives
When we need to learn to forgive...
But how do I do that when you
Have taken so much from me...
You changed my life forever
In ways you'll never understand
You left me bruised and broken...
You walked away untouched
Not so much as a word from you
To find out how my recovery is progressing
So I'll let you know...
I am taking baby steps in my
New journey of life...
And I know that someday
With God's help...
I will be able to say to you,
"I forgive you"

Linda Elmquist
Johnsonburg, PA

It's Only in Dreams: Sonnet of Sorrow

It's only in dreams that the legless man runs,
Jumps and dances like the other ones—
It's only in dreams that the mute man speaks
And the lonely man finds the love he seeks—
It's only in dreams that the sick get well,
Where their daily life is no living hell—
It's only in dreams that the poor have much more,
Where their debts don't crush them to the floor—
It's only in dreams that the ugly girl is pretty,
Where boys offer her something more than pity
Sadly, in real life the world is lacking
And reality is busy with our joy attacking—
It's hard to be happy for those of human breath
And the crimes of life only end with death

Leo Weber
Livonia, MI

What Happened to the Good Old USA?

What happened to the good old USA?
When people came to visit and some would want to stay.
When people had jobs and homes, it was the American dream,
In the good old USA.

When children used to go outside to play, and not sit in the house
    all day.
When we were free to pledge allegiance to the flag.
And race and color were the same.

When the laws were written for the criminals and no one else.
And congress was for the people and not for themselves.
When women were women and men were men,
And they knew the difference then.

And they all stood tall and strong to the very end.
What happened to the good old USA?
What happened to the country I love and was proud to say,
I'm from the good old USA?
We lost our manor, respect and dignity and now we got shame.
What happened to the good old USA?

Gloria Esperanza
Sun Valley, NV

Conundrum

Through thick and thin, I stuck with you
and this is what I get?
Heart broken beyond repair
and mind: full of regret.

As days drag to night
and I lay in my bed
I know sleep won't come
because you're in my head.

Your sweet, loving voice
and your tenderest touch:
I try to forget them,
they just hurt too much.

Mind and body, heart and soul,
I gave myself to you.
I guess that that was just too much
you didn't know what to do.

You led me on one day
and shunned me the next.
Some days I felt blessed
and the next I felt vexed.

You left me here bleeding,
a hole in my chest,
and yet I still love you,
still wish you the best.

Tiffany Knox
Laval, QC

Oh Darkest Night

And so now we start again
To pray and wish for us to win,
A life we've longed to start anew,
To spend forever now with you.

From when I stepped out to the light,
Always wishing for you at night,
The pain and tear I had to beat,
For it's my heart I could not cheat!

The dragging of each dying day,
I could only dream of you to stay.
My heart would cry a moment's fear,
But my soul cries out in silent tear.

I dread the days of longest wait.
I'm always left in a wondering state.
Looking forward to be with you,
I wish it now, I wish I knew…

Every prayer I seize to do.
I ask above to be with you!
I recite them all each day.
I wish my love forever stay.

The longing of each dying night
I wish it may I wish with might.
There in my dream I'd rather be,
For in my dreams you are with me!

Carolyn Hines
Rosemead, CA

Rain Check

Those clouds, darkest midnight blue
Against the dawn,
Promise a heavy load
Of something very cold
Later on.

A lone cyclist winks by
And the park is mine again.
All the lights are on,
But the only heat
Emanates from me,
And a bitter wind,
With a dry kiss,
Fingers it away.

It's a half-mile trek to collect
An *Oregonian*, a cardboard cuppa joe,
A scone, a morning, "Hello,"
Then, quick, back across the park.
A sudden needle of sun
Separates the clouds,
Announcing more to come
Than just that icy
Silver-bullet rain.

Eleanor Malin
Portland, OR

I'm a caregiver, a breadwinner, a writer, a good employee, and a moral person, and in spite of all that, I have a pretty good sense of humor. I guess I would have to. Anyway, I do as much as I can, as often as I can, and try to be as reasonable and fair with myself as I am to everyone else. Eleanor Malin, born in LaCrosse, WI, a long time ago, is currently a citizen/taxpayer in Portland, Oregon.

The Essentials

Let the fantasies of my life
revive me
and the dreams of my heart
survive me.
The loves of my life
sustain me —
temptations never to conquer me,
nor test me beyond strength
to endure them
that I may ever cling to truth
whilst fulfilling in me,
the "I am" that lives and breathes
and has its very indwelling —
the ever surviving soul —
creates and encompasses me.

Anna Louise Greenmun
Glendale, AZ

Our Wealth

All of glory
none of betrayal
life's meaning
if met two to tango
no oaf
be my mercies
for goodness not lost
yet of our banner
so long ago
that freedom flies
prevail spirit
afford this tribute
oh mercy no
left alone
I can't waive
nor lay
this fight awoke
our wealth
last strong

Rene Volpe
Branford, CT

This poem is dedicated to family members that have passed away.

A Night to Remember

It was a Friday evening
at the ballroom dance
When we first met
a night I'll never forget
You came and said,
May I have this dance
You held me close
As we moved cross
The floor
I looked at you and
I thought could he
be the one I've been
waiting for
A love song was
playing
You held me closer
my heart skipped
a beat
you are beautiful
I love you
I sighed and replied
softly, I love you too
In that moment we
both knew we would
always be together
our whole life through

Ruth C. Noga
East Pointe, MI

A Kind of Sadness

Mid-August predawn
It's quiet here
I lie awake
A scent of lilac
Fills the room
Wistful, it's feel
Time passes on the clock
Outside the elm
Is grand and tall
The wooden swing
Hangs empty
And memories pervade
I gaze upward
Toward the sky
It's clear; the stars are bright
A yellow moon looks down
As if to offer empathy
To me and to the world
And the catbird sings!

Bobbie Morris
Swarthmore, PA

The last five lines are a kind of metaphor for those who extended deep empathy and caring to me while at a very "low" time in my life.

Spiritual Meadows

As I walk with you, Lord,
I seek mountain meadows
dotted with wildflowers
bathed in sunshine.
But, walking with you, Lord,
day by day
includes the flat, hot deserts,
the dark, shaded valleys,
the steep, rocky hills
that occasionally
lead to mountain meadows
filled with flowers and sunshine.

Jane Williams
Athens, OH

Unmisunderstood

Unconfused
Uncollected
Untold
Unnew
Unfold
Untrue
Absolute and true
What more can we do?
The flying time
The waiting line
The unmisunderstood truths
The fears of expression
The burning passions
The unspoken words
The relenting unconfused
A state which stays stagnant
The moment is inevitable to pass
If this direction remains unpassed
What more is there to do?
The word must be spoken, but expressed with truth and sincerity
What more is there to do to break the stagnation of the
    misunderstood?
The truths, the fears of expression, the burning passions,
the unspoken words, the relenting unconfused?
Tell me what more is there to do?
It's really always been waiting on you

Lillian Strom
Huntington Beach, CA

Is This What We Really Need

Love, love, love
Is that what we really need?

The Beatles' song says that is all we need
Is it all we really need
I say yes, it is
Our maker gave us the keys to paradise
Saying, "Love one another"
Only we didn't know these words are the keys

Love, love, love
That is all we need
If we practiced it would the world be able
To sustain those who die from wars
Street wars, family wars, world wars and wars in the
Heart of an individual who is consumed with hate
As hate eats at the soul, disease wears the body
And soul to nothing

Our creator created us to be something, not nothing
So practice love unconditionally
Love, yes, that's all we need
Unconditionally!

Barbara Goldson
Davie, FL

Marching Band

The pulsing beat
The sound of drums
Sweat wiped from a brow
Sore muscles
And sunburned skin,
Straight backs
And echoing laughs
The chaos of sound
Coming together,
Woodwind and brass
It takes more than an individual,
It takes individuals working together
To form a band
The bond formed
Will forever have a pull,
An automatic tug
To those fond memories
Time spent
And connections forged,
Grime, sweat, and tears
Poured out on a field,
For those minutes of utter focus
And that final moment
Of complete accomplishment

Aisha Hellman-Lohr
Austin, TX

Nature's Beauty

The trees are full of leaves
Green and lush
The flowers are fully bloomed
The fruit sweet, almost heavenly.

This time of year
Love is in bloom
The kisses sweet, like wine
Fully lush and blushing
The kisses so sweet,
And full of passion
This side of Heaven

The feeling of strength and gentleness
When he holds you,
The feeling of safety
When he lets you be you.

There's always sunshine and rain;
Can't have one without the other.
The sunshine's brightness feeds our soul.
The rain fuels our body.
They both fuel our heart.

Yes, this time of year, everything's in bloom.

Sharon A. Denney
Mechanicville, NY

'Round and About

Ancient places sit quietly by the bay
swallowing time with nothing
interrupting—today
every window looks out at magnificent views
hawks fly soaring
as if awaiting the news
long tables wait at attention until dawn
chipped dishes sit on shelves
expecting company now gone
...until holidays bring laughter
and life throughout...
these ancient places surround our hearts
'round 'round and about...

JoAnne Deslauriers
Acushnet, MA

The Room

I.   The room, as I recall
Is a place with a secret door
Where the pressure of daily living
Doesn't bother you anymore.

II.   All your troubles and your cares
Seem to float away with the evening tide
No stress, no crazy people, nothing scary
In that room trying to hide.

III. This room is filled with happiness
As I can see from the smile on your face
You've traveled back and forth through time
Trying to reach your happy place.

IV. This room has an ocean view
White glass, white walls in your reoccurring dream
This may be your idea of Heaven
Filled with love, peaches, and cream.

V.   I don't recall you mentioning others
Being allowed to enjoy your fun
Not one word about a friend with you
Enjoying the beach and sun.

VI. Well that's okay, as long as you
Are having the time of your life
A warm summer breeze caressing your soul
With love, with hope, and without strife.

Andre Patterson
Gadsden, AL

You Are Alive and Well, Enjoy Your Life

Where is the fun we used to have in the days of our youth, has
it disappeared forever in the mist of our dreams? Remember
the real feelings that we had for one another,
I feel that you are lying to me, for you know what I mean.
Is this the year of our dismissal of hurt feelings and shame?

You are the doubter of all that is pure and solid in life.
Can you not see the reasons that I care for you so much?
I forever see the things that make you hesitate to seek out.
While you are asleep, things around you tend to slip away.

Only you need to see with your eyes the beauty of life.
Give someone the beauty of your knowledge of things.
Take ahold of your devils and shake them from your mind,
To be solid in your heart is the big difference of your faith.

You shall overcome all your misgivings of the sounds by
Kissing your hand and saying "I love me" for it won't hurt.
Smile a smile for all to see and dwell in its warmness,
For you are someone with pride, take it and live happy.

Once again, you have the look of blissful connections,
Your eyes have that mystic sparkle of happiness in them.
There is a stairway to the stars, rise up and take it happily,
For you are alive and well, enjoy your life as days go by.

Jerry T. Freeman
Lake City, AR

A Place Called Home

Home is where you wander
over fields, meadows and streams.

Home is where the birds sing
their sweetness above your head.

Home is where your brightest
dreams can come true.

It's memories of Mom and Dad
and childhood too.

It's not a place just where you
eat and sleep.

A home that's real has something
that's lovable and sweet.

It may be a cottage or a castle
in Spain.

But with love and honor life
won't be in vain.

Jewell Roper
Cullman, AL

Quincy

Uncle Mike's dog Quincy
When he comes running to you
Panting, out of breath
He won't bite you
But just lick you to death.
If he's sleepy, he's in a cranky mood,
But he's not picky about his food.
Quincy is named after Quincy Street.
To find another dog like Quincy
Would be hard to beat.
He adores his master Uncle Michael.
Mike doesn't have him on an obedience cycle.
Quincy has a mind of his own;
He will stay that way, even when he's grown.
He chases squirrels all over the yard
And acts like he is always on guard.
He is lovable like a child,
Sometimes he's hyper and sometimes he's mild.
Quincy has dog bones all over the house,
And likes to hunt bugs, snails, and even a mouse.

Ruby V. Hyatt
Elmendorf, TX

Longest River

Being alone is not all that great.
No one wants someone who's not first rate.
You have to fill your days with whatever,
And hope you are not headed down the longest river.

You turn to God and you pray hard.
You keep going but, you're so tired.
Everyone says you should stop and pray,
But when you do, no answers come your way.

Your faith is getting weaker and weaker.
You are wondering if God is your seeker.
What to do, to turn this life of yours around,
And give a chance of your faith to be found.

You keep on praying until your word is heard by God.
He says, I give you comfort by my staff and my rod.
So you go on and take one day at a time.
Your life goes on like a flowing river of wine.

But, if your life does stand still for a short while,
It's time to pray, renew faith and smile,
That someone is here in this life to remind us we will not fail.
We have a purpose and someone cares to no avail.

So the loneliness is not cured, it still comes and goes,
But my faith is a little bit stronger and life seems to have less woes.
Hour by hour, day by day, we turn to God to show us the way,
Because no matter what we do the river still flows day after day.

Rebecca De Loof
Battle Creek, MI

Close to You

No one would guess who took his place,
Because he left me unnoticed.
Now I can't find my happiness,
I am tormented, broken in two.

But then I see the others' torments,
I may share some sympathy.
I will forget the hurt I have,
And I will find some things to see.

Throughout these days of sadness,
A little creature came into my life.
He is so gentle and oh so white,
He is now what I have to love.

He took his place, he showed his love,
He can't speak but sings a lot.
He made me laugh and feel secure,
Just by making himself so close.

Don't be surprised, he is a bird
A bird we hatched and cared.
Pixie sings, he flies, and even cheers,
His melodious whistle captures my heart.

Yes, he is a white, tamed cockatiel
We all love him with all our hearts.
He belongs to us, in our life,
A family member close to my heart.

Aniceta P. Alcayaga
San Diego, CA

What Time Is Love?

What time is love
Be kind to love
I don't mind love
Being everywhere at once

I'll love you till
Times Square forgets
How to bring in the New Year
I'll love you till
The Dallas Cowgirls forget
How to cheer

I'll love you till
The honky-tonks
All run out of beer
I'll love you till
God tells me not to
My dear

Roy A. Smith
West Columbia, SC

Power(less) Memories

Some are dark; some are bathed in heavenly light
Some draw tears from evil fears others call forth faith
Feeling proud, ashamed, full of joy or spite
Opening wounds, tearing apart seams, leaving skaith

Time is endless, time is fleeting
Seconds tick to minutes, minutes turn to hours
No reason to waste years aiming to be deleting
Moments that age faster than those weeded flowers

Youth is foolish, void of wisdom's learning
Wisdom is infallible, but ever taunted in wraith
Confidence is a poison when doubts are discerning
Whether it's the first year or the ninety-eighth

Some days smiles fleeting as snowflakes over flames
We find friends are fickle as fair-weather
Memories pour in like salt to an open wound, never tame
Binding fast like a chain, or tether

Darkness may cloud the light, eclipses happen in shade
Fuzzy minds crumple under strain, resisting destruction
Time is endless; so shed the stones so heavily weighed
For memories sweet or sour act only as obstructions

Jessica Thayer
Brockton, MA

If

I eat, I sleep, I dream, I daydream, I study, I worship,
I idolize the color green as in tea-green. Green in all my ways was I,
'cause if I knew then what I know now. I am neither
innocent nor guilty but neutral within the confines of my
passion. Such was my lot.
Cannot muse over what might have been. What has been will have
no effect on what will happen, I theorize.
Should have taken pathway's charm. It is what it is. Do tell!
That mighty if word with many meanings.
If the stars and water and numbers don't lie, why should I?
If the glitterin' mass of stars avail.
I danced with melancholy and discontent in the first hours;
I danced in the last hours, 'til no more hours were left in the day.
And endless days and sleepless nights, my dry bones and dry bread.
Then came you springin' up like a tulip, freein' me from
my inhibitions,
the start of something afresh and anew. And how and why we met.
And the bright mornin' star. Do let!
A thousand kisses will suffice. A thousand kisses at that.
Our terms of endearment.
But we danced a greater dance, a meaningful dance, a happy dance;
and playful days and peaceful nights.
And we danced many times more, 'til we danced no more.
Then you became my ghost, leavin' me frozen in time.
I stood still as a statue, askin', "Why?"
If time would but allow me to write and rewrite its chronicles,
I would, 'til no more time was left in a day. But it won't. Do show!
Do embrace the inevitable! Do accept the unacceptable!
If I could have but another chance, a mere chance, a golden chance,
a random chance, a major chance, per chance, par chance, half a
chance, take back all my chances…'til we meet again.

Reginald W. Murray
Philadelphia, PA

The Spider

It's simply amazing, that one sticky thread
Can be spun by a spider to create her web
Shimmering ladders lead to her domain
She waits there with hunger, her victim to claim.

Along comes a spider with amorous intent,
She stays on her throne as she savors the scent
That wafts to her olfactory nerves, on the breeze.
"I'll get him!" she vows, "I'll bring him to his knees!"

Oh innocent victim, if only you knew
That others have been through this ordeal too
And ended, a dastardly death to endure
As the Queen of the Web made her banquet secure.

This one's no exception, and after they mate
This carnivorous female lets him meet his fate.
The web looked attractive all dappled with dew
A thing of great beauty and delicate too.

Oh learn from the spider, this truth I will tell
So often the pathway to fun leads to Hell!

Heather Mairn Owen
Lakeville, MN

The Distance

How far away do you have to be before you feel alone?
How close together some people are and still feel alone.
The distance between us can be miles or days.
It's what's in your heart that makes it this way.
Family and friends should all get along.
How many times has this gone wrong?
It starts without warning, nobody tells you about it.
The distance starts to grow and there is nothing you can do about it.
You let some things go and others you do not.
The simplest things can tie you in knots!
Closing the distance is the simplest of all.
If we work together, we are sure not to fall.
How the heart aches when distance is near.
Yet we go there often and swallow our fear.

Lori Oberman
Sparks, NV

Robin Williams and Me

I loathe to be alone again
As in the womb
Not knowing where I've been
Or even now am yet to go

This shell of flesh bears down
Upon my tethered soul
And makes my solitary life
A loathsome lie

My memories, the hopes of future dreams,
Flow without joy or peace now that
My life has been laid bare
And hope has lost its grip

Like driftwood in a rushing stream
Worn down and brittle
Without a destination
Finally washing ashore to be
Buried in the sand

Everyone blames me
But why do I blame myself
With no choice
But to be born

Too early will I take my pills
And go to bed and just forget
Better to sleep than kill myself
When all I want is to be dead

Carol M. Heineman
Lehigh Acres, FL

I've lost everything except the depression, a lifelong companion. Life can be cruel. Depression is worse. The demons in your head, just chemicals, make every day a battle, but it's a battle you must win. My weapons? Swimming laps, Journey to the Heart *by Melody Beattie—life changing, a mood light—also miraculous, and my anchor and friend, Jesus. Prayer is not the last resort. It's the most powerful weapon of all, and the Bible is sharper than any two-edged sword. No kidding! I've made it sixty-four years. I like my odds.*

Memento Mori

Last night I dreamed about him
in his hospital bed,
unbearably frail next to the machines
that broadcasted how slowly he will recover.
My dream self tried to rest a hand on his forearm
only to have it pass through
his skin and broken bones;
it was impossible to tell
which of us was the intangible one.
I kept trying to touch him
and could only watch my hand sink.
I watched him breathe shallow
until the hospital room dissolved
into my bedroom
where I must pace and wait.

After last year's accident,
I sat on the sidewalk
where I swore I could still see
remnants of teeth
reminding me that
only fragments had been lost.

I have nowhere to mourn
his blood, the nerves in his arm and leg.
The fresh stains on the sidewalk are 3,000 miles away.

Claire McDonald
Oakland, CA

If I Followed My Heart

If I followed my heart, I'd be where you are
If I followed my heart, I'd text, "Good morning beautiful," daily
If I followed my heart, I'd call just to hear your sweet voice
If I followed my heart, I'd dance with you often
If I followed my heart, I'd hold you in my arms just because
If I followed my heart, I'd be content with you leading
If I followed my heart, I'd live the reality instead of dreaming
If I followed my heart, you'd know you had me wrapped around
   your finger at first sight
If I followed my heart, I'd plant soft kisses on you sporadically
If I followed my heart, we'd walk hand-n-hand during our after
   dinner strolls
If I followed my heart, I'd close my eyes and hold on tight during
   bike riding Sunday
If I followed my heart, I'd protect you forever and ever
If I followed my heart, you would complete me
If I followed my heart, I'd be so happy
If I followed my heart...
But I won't dare

Nicole Rochelle Duckery
Philadelphia, PA

Have to Let You Grow Now

Close to four years I have succumbed to—
your indecision of being my friend
Your partner held me at bay…
I knocked in friendship,
she was made of clay
Judged me and forced me away—
rude; her voice cold as ice
A cup of tea, maybe a simple chat?
An iron cross she wore and built the negative wall
I went away and cared, no more
No more knocks and ceased to call
To assisted living she went—why should I care
Why should I dare to try to befriend you—sympathy and time spent?
The season? The reason?
She is gone now…
In your sorrow and grief—my belief—
to shelter the twenty-eight years the two of you shared
From your drunken mouth you spout,
"We were doing fine until you arrived!"
and yet you beckon me to be near and dear
In your loss and in your heart?
It's time to part… comes another to fill your void, your empty space
I feel the time we've shared you will replace
The adage goes, "A friend in need is a friend indeed,"
and so I was

Nancy L. Cox
Denver, CO

When My Soul Is Asleep

Where I walk there is
Magic in the sand
Where I linger there are
Shadows where I stand
When I cry there are
Reflections in my eyes
When I pray there are
No lies
When I dream, memories are
Not cast aside
When my tears fall they are
Washed away with the tide
Where I lay, my soul
Is to keep
It's in heavenly hands when
My soul is asleep

Diana L. Davis
Ft. Lauderdale, FL

Moments of You

Your physical presence
The touch of your hands
A dance — a soft caress
A gentle kiss
Your laughter — your smile
When you whisper in my ear
Sitting on the dryer
When you say, "I love you"
The way you look at me
When you pull my body close to yours…
These are the tender moments
I treasure with you…
The moments of love

Carol D. Brewer
Pomona, CA

I have been writing poetry for over forty years. Within the last three years, I've experienced a love like no other, a love that really allows me to go deep within myself and write about love. This poem was inspired by my friend of fifty-plus years. He has been my good friend since 1962, when we were teenagers. We have since re-acquainted, in the last three years. He inspires me to write from deep within my heart. He inspires me to feel love, like never before, and for that, I am grateful for this experience.

Strong

Be thankful for what is around you
See the trees blowing in the wind
Smell the aroma of flowers
Soaking it all in

Everything is peaceful
You watch the small birds fly
Life is a blessing
Don't let it pass you by

The clouds quickly turn grey
Your world becoming dark
Rain starts to pour
There is an ache in your heart

You feel lost on this planet
There is no right turn
But please do not go
You have so much left to learn

As life goes on
The sky will become bright
Your smile will return
You've had a long hard fight

You've overcome obstacles
Feeling now like you belong
You are forever free
You are forever strong

Allison Sorrell
Kenton, MB

Easy Down

Life hurts and it's scary
Prices are high and I'm feeling low
How can I not be so weary
So that this day can just let me go
I should be winding down and not
Pushing it on fast forward
To be on top of things now and
Turning them to come about from
Being inward
Is it this way or that way
Who's who in this zoo?!
We came a long way to be
Winners not losers to cry
Boo hoo
Young or old changes are made
Without being right or wrong
Until finding out this is not the
Place to talk about it like you hear
In a song
Time goes by so fast I don't know
How it catches up to me like it does
Because of doing one thing or another
I can't face the time as it was
I'm a poet and didn't know it

Mary S. Osborne
Jamestown, NY

A Rose Past Its Prime

I have walked down this street before with you
All talked out for old time's sake yet striving
To hoard the remnants of a budding love
Past the prime of youth spent.

I told you sos and could haves, should haves,
Would haves, maybes abound as we wrestle
To place blame at the feet of each other
For the demise of a once special relationship.

Having told me once that I knew you better
It has become clear that I don't know you at all
For you are as removed from me as the Crete Indians
From which I descend!

Why hold onto fleeting bits and pieces of stems
Protruding from the vine shrivelled
When it is better to walk on in the world alone
As a new rose blooms.

Cleo E. Brown
New York, NY

My name is Cleo E. Brown. I have a bachelor's degree in history and political science from California State University at Stanislaus and a master's degree from UC Davis. I have also worked on a PhD in education from the University of San Francisco. To date I have published four books of poems: For Steven, Tears Shed for Gustavo, Life Cycles *and* Only a Woman. *I have also published a book of history and political science titled* In Search of the Republican Party: A History of Minorities in the Republican Party. *Currently, I live in Manhattan, New York.*

Greek God

There is something about your white smile and those baby blues
That leave big butterflies in girls stomachs and weak in the knees
Your ego grew and grew as you lied and cheated
Got away with it all never mattered how many girls you mistreated

Still females lined up to take their shot in hopes to be undefeated
A fight never won with each new girl that came the other got deleted
Your reputation grew; no doubt you were considered a Greek god
Males look up to you; to them you were a legend that they all applaud

Despite the warnings, I caught myself falling for you hard
It didn't matter how much I try; you defiantly caught me off guard
I thought I knew what to expect as your reputation became clear
But instead you were honest with me, you washed away all of
　my fears

When I was with you, I never had to fake a smile
Sweet kisses that caught my breath my heart raced for miles
It never mattered what happened, you always told the truth
You did the sweetest things and I knew I had the proof

You are not cold hearted as everyone made you out to be
You are always doing everything in your power by watching over me
You are smart and have a lot of insight
No matter how hard things got you never gave up the fight

My life, my heart and my soul will never be the same
After being with you; the smile still remains
It's a shame that we did drift apart
But I hope you know you will always hold a small piece of my heart

Lisa Carr
St. Albert, AB

Jersey Shore

Seaside Heights is always home
Regardless of the roads I roam.
The sand, the bay, the ocean blue
I will always remember you.
The breathtaking sunsets on Normandy Bay
Acted as closure from nature each day.
Best part of all was the boardwalk at night
Smells of salt water and moon shining bright.
Suddenly it ended by Hurricane Sandy
No more rides, games or shops, no pink cotton candy.
My home is now gone but I'll always remember
The time of my life from May to September.

Laurie Jogan
Winter Park, FL

The Generations

He looks somewhat like Grandpa,
That tasseled head of hair,
A lopsided grin, the laughter.
They make quite a pair.
He mimics Grandpa's walk.
Holds tight to his hand
Feeling the strength of generations.
Sharing is part of their plan.

Loraine Faschingbauer
Bloomer, WI

In My Lifetime

How heavenly life would be
without the pain and without the sorrow,
without the fear and without the angst,
without the tears and without the regrets.
No more shame. No more despair. No more greed. No more guilt.
End the famine. End the war. Undo the discriminations. Eliminate
   the segregations.
Abolish the abuse. Dismiss the stress. Soothe the mind. Calm
   the soul.
Oh, why can't we all see
how heavenly life would be.

Diana Richardson
Yonkers, NY

The Afghan War: Summer of 2010

Children come to plant the bombs,
Fooled by their deadly dreams.
Clerics spin their hollow tales,
Of holy wars and infidels.

Limp and lonely limbs lay still,
Among the blood fed reeds.
Bullets whiz by our heads,
As shrapnel serves for seeds.

Clouds of dust stir from the ground,
To cover the sun's bright glow.
Blackened smoke smolders in the sky.
No answer to our frantic, "Why?"

Flag covered coffins disembark,
From the mouths of yawning hawks.
Tears wash the faces of our birth,
Like salted rain on stunted earth.

Patricia E. Christie-Brooks
Manchester, CT

Patricia Christie-Brooks is a sixty-eight-year-old grandmother who retired from her position as a State of CT civil rights investigator. Her poetry and other writings have been included in anthropology, memoir, and poetry journals. She has published three books. She included this poem, "The Afghan War: Summer of 2010," to refresh our memory of what failed diplomacy and subsequently another war in the Middle East would mean in 2015 and beyond.

My Son!

Who is this child
Who is my son?
I think of him when the day is done.
How the years have flown,
He's now a man.
Thoughtful, kind, the best I've known.

As I think of days when he was small,
Never dreaming he'd hear the call
To serve his country, proud and true,
Defending it for me and you!
Always helpful, my little man,
He always seemed to understand.
He has two little girls, a wife so true,
All with golden hair, eyes of blue.
He always seems to think of me
When I'm feeling blue, he calls me!
When I hear him say, "I love you, Mom,"
It's worth all the gold in the land!

Sharon R. Bauer
Edgemont, SD

The Poet

I am but a poor and lowly poet,
Looked upon as strange by my peers.
If they but had the wisdom and courage
They could see beyond their fears.
I have this and other talents
Of which I am very proud,
And someday soon I hope to see
Others like me in a crowd.
I have no money to speak of,
But still I'm very rich,
Because I have all nature gives
In my own little niche.
I have words of silver and gold
To slip right off my pen,
And arrange themselves in verses bold,
Thus a beautiful poem begins.
I try to see the world
Through the verses in my mind,
And I write from experiences
My life has chanced to find.
My writing comes from within.
The emotions of my soul
Spill forth in flowing melodies,
And the poem takes control.

Barbara E. Selby
Waycross, GA

Inquiry of Time

Time:
That is the ultimate force,
Which controls, consumes, destroys…
A devil in the making, it eats up your soul
Until you are nothing but rotting flesh and bones
Buried in the ground.
Literally.
Think about it.
What would happen if time didn't exist?
The world would be in bliss,
Completely oblivious to the idea of being early…
Or worse, late…
Or worst of all dead or alive…
For how could one gauge birth or death without the master of time?
And that my friend, is why time even exists!
It is an immortal evil. Yes. But it is also a necessary blessing.
So, let the clocks tick on, and the rhythms of timers chime.
Now if you'll excuse me, I have a date with time.

Samyuktha Ravikumar
Irvine, CA

Samyuktha Ravikumar is an aspiring contemporary poet. She has been an avid writer since the age of eight, when she wrote her first poem. Samyuktha's poems are usually very heartfelt. Most of them describe emotional moments such as the birth of a baby or the loss of a treasured pet. These poems have touched the hearts of many people and have helped them open their eyes to new worlds. As she continues on in her career, Samyuktha hopes to experiment with new styles of writing and explore new subjects along the way.

Five Little Girls

Five little girls and how they grew.
Some folks said they made quite a crew.

But Dad didn't seem to care,
He had no son to be his heir.
He often boasted with a grin,
That Eddie Cantor had nothing on him.

Of course, they had their little spats,
Chasing each other around like little cats.
Then when things got a little rough,
Mom would say, "Now, that's enough."

They never got bored like kids today.
They always found some game to play.

They all grew up to be proper young ladies,
All got married and had lots of babies.
Now Dad is a very proud grandfather,
With more grandsons than granddaughters.

Erna Wolfe
Columbus, NE

Faith First

Have faith in the Lord, be washed in his blood.
Receive his understanding, feel the power in his love.
Walk ever so carefully, plant your feet on solid ground.
Tread lightly, through his holy Bible,
And listen to every sound.
For one can hear and see, many events that took place.
From the dawn of time,
To the end, which will soon take place.
You can see and feel, the evening our Savior was born.
The cold starry night, the stable, and the three wise men.
Or of Adam and Eve, when one son, killed the other.
What paid and grief was suffered,
First time, by a father and a mother.
Or that sorrowful eve, when Jesus died on the cross.
But this he had to do,
The price, for the sins of the lost.
Or of David, facing Goliath, pitting a stone,
Against a sword. Or of Daniel, in the lion's den,
Putting his faith all in the Lord.
Or of a time to come, when the righteous are raptured.
And of the loved ones left behind,
To suffer, and face God's judgement.
Read and believe, for what is written,
Paves the road for your victory.
With your sons, forgiven.

Lawrence Melvin
Greenup, KY

My Mornings

I take a walk each morning
    before the daylight breaks,
I smell so many scents,
    that are present everywhere
The smell of coffee brewing
    the bacon and the rest
The sounds of all the vehicles
    being started for the day,
The train with all its cargo,
    tooting on its way,
The birdies chirping music,
    With all the sounds they make —
The dogs and cats are resting
    lazy on the grass —
I raise my head to Heaven
    as I walk along my path,
And I thank our Lord each morning
    for all the things he sends

Gloria Rosas Maldonado
Kingsville, TX

I love to write poems. My loved ones love to read them. My family consists of: husband Guadalupe; son Rudy and wife Sylvia; grandchildren Melanie, Stephanie, Natalie, Rudy Jr., and Valarie; great-grandchildren Alyssa, Daisy, Adrian, Eric, Aiden, Emily, Andrew, Isabella, and Abigail; parents Mamerto and Juanita Rosas; siblings Mario Perez, Juanita Antonia, San Juanita Barerra, Consuelo Vilches, Mamerto Jr., Juventino, Cristoval, and Manuelito Rosas; and many nieces and nephews. From my parents I learned love, respect, labor, education, sharing, religion and to be honest. This will be my fourth poem published.

Apathy

Spreading disease
And dying bees
Are signs of ending times;
You cry about your issues
And I hand you some tissues
While they scrape away our minds.
If it looks good in theory
Then it must be alright.
We're losing all our freedom
While they're "giving us our rights."
Conform or be lost in the dark of night.
Prepare to ignore the coming fight.

They're saving trees,
But killing babies,
We sit here apathetic.
Find perfect justification
For our passive situation
When it should be called pathetic.
If no one finds this wrong
Then we're stupid together.
We're a nation of sheep
Being led on a tether,
Responding to tragedy with: "Whatever."
The choices we make affect us forever.

Elisabeth Eye
Coolville, OH

PCH

That year I step by step
And in your mind think years,
Here another year and step
To the top called "PCH"!

But what do three letters mean,
A star in the sky, a virtual planet?!
At night I roam the "Milky Way,"
Looking for a mysterious "PCH"!

I'm not the only one in America,
There are millions of white, black, yellow!
And we all pray to the "idol"
And all waiting for a miracle!

Comes regular mail from "PCH"
And we wonder "Shakespeare":
"To be or not to be" this time?!
And sticking stamps on destiny!

Maybe we didn't win a million,
And got just a cheap package,
Anyway we are always happy
Our mysterious "Publishers Clearing House"!

Because our "PCH" is not just a house,
But a corporation of wonderful people,
Which gives us very important feelings:
Saints Faith, Hope and Love!

Kazbek M. Tuayev
W Sacramento, CA

I was born on July 9, 1936, in the city Vladikavkaz, Russia, into the family of a Baptist pastor. My father died in the Soviet camp, while my mother died from heavy suffering and stress. Since my childhood, I have dreamed of writing. I write mostly in Russian and a little bit in English. Also, I have collaborated with Publishers Clearing House (PCH) for many years. It is a very interesting business and I invite everybody!

Snares

Beware! The devil has a special snare —
"Don't scoff" — it's very true.
How he'd like to get right in,
And make a mess of you!

He makes you think that wrong is right —
Turns your day to blackest night.

Twists your soul and blinds your sight —
Then tries to tell you it's all right.

A liar and a cheat he is —
That's why the world's a mess —
He's blinded eyes and hardened hearts —
So people won't confess.

He hates the ones for whom Christ died —
Wrecks their lives, and makes them cry.

He gives a snare of "porn" or "rum" —
It's different, friend, for everyone.
Some get "blue" jokes and puns —
He'll never talk of God's own Son!

He wants you to believe his lies —
And keeps you very occupied —
Until at last your life is done —
He's on his way to another one.

Be not decided by any "snare" —
He wants to throw your way.
There's not a time he ever cared —
He'll rot in hell — let him go there!

Janice Olli
Hancock, MI

Don't Oxygen Me Out!

My body is a broken home on a land filled with dust.
The frame is my statue leaning to one side.
The boards are decayed like my vertebrae.
The closed shutters are my lungs coughing with debris.
The cracks on the walls are knives in my heart from a distant love.
The note on the doorsteps is a burst vein in my leg.
Nighttime is near overshadowing the darkness in my eyes.
I can no longer see happiness.

Millette Roberson
Richmond, TX

Writing poetry is Millette's passion. It gives her such pride and joy sharing this artistic vision to the world. She was born in Houston, Texas. She attended Texas Southern University and graduated with a bachelor of business administration. She furthered her education by receiving a master of education from Grand Canyon University in Arizona. She has written several published poems and nominated as Poet of the Year 2002. She is a widow who resides in Richmond, Texas, with her three beautiful children: daughter Millicent and sons Prince and Kennedy.

The Newtons

I have these friends named Newtons,
Wayne Ann and Charlie are great!
Our friendship goes far back,
The rest is nothing but fate.
The roots were from a business,
John and Charlie were always there.
Scheffel and Lyman were part of it,
Their friendship was very rare.
As years went by too fast,
Time consuming kids were born.
No time to fraternize a lot,
And no time to sit and mourn.
Since we're in the fall of life,
It's time to live a little.
Love you both so very much,
Come to the "Village" and "Fiddle"!

Yvonne K. Hoefert
Godfrey, IL

*The mother of six, grandmother of nineteen and great-grandmother of two
all living within four miles, I am the widow of my "hero," John W. Hoefert
Sr. I just sold my home in six weeks and moved to a retirement apartment. I
couldn't be happier. Soon to turn eighty-five, I had a cocktail party for some
friends. They range in ages from seventy-five to ninety-three. One couple said
I never wrote about them so the following day I wrote "The Newtons."*

Head Shrinker

They say by reducing the size of your hat
You will understand the abstract
And you will feel better, be thankful for that

We will fill your head full of juice
Hang on to the table your head's coming loose
They say by reducing the size of your hat

And with each seizure your mind should improve
We know you have trouble each time that you move
And you will feel better, be thankful for that

These pills that we give you should help you rest
When you remember you once were the best
They say by reducing the size of your hat

Within our hotel you're a special guest
Some of the patients will be your pests
And you will feel better, be thankful for that

And when you are crazy and can't take any more
We will throw you into a room on the floor
By the time you leave you'll be as crazy as a bat
They say by reducing the size of your hat
And you will feel better, be thankful for that

Kenneth Hinkle
Winchester, VA

Rain Desperation

Will it ever rain again?
The earth needs washing, the flowers need hydrating
The heart of the sun is burdensome
No snow will come when winter does
Not on this golden coast
The sun would not help enhance the holiday atmosphere
December would not be complete
Without curling on the couch with a hot cup of cider
Fall is nearly here and the chance for rain is slim
The ground is hard and packed dry
Sooner or later this drought will end
Clouds! Bring your fireworks show
And with your thunderous trumpets
Announce the need for umbrellas
And, most of all—please bring the rain

JaNeli Holladay
Fremont, CA

Each Common Thing

Lord may I never grow too old to find
In life, each common thing a joy
Deep seated peace and beauty, for the mind
Is likened to a weaver that employs
Rich colors for the pattern he was wrought
Until at last his work complete, he knows
The satisfied expression of a thought
For beauty that we cherish slowly grows
From the thoughts that only loveliness can bring
Throughout the long entanglement of years
It lifts the spirit up on golden wings
In simple, quiet things, no room for tears
But with a life enriched by thoughts of love
Find peace and strength drawn down from heights above

Ruth Thorud
Eden Prairie, MN

Elm

Quietly sitting looking at the stars
Mind slowly drifts, but not too far
Remembering a time with my mom
A smile, a hug and oh the charm
A strong woman who taught me well
With a firm hand and love that was swell
Every minute of the day,
I miss her in every way
Especially the month of her birth
Unconditional love my heart has searched
Mother's love is untouched
Freely given with hugs, kisses and such
Yes, she taught me how to go on
Knowing she had to meet the number one father and son
Now with her guidance gone
For many a year, my trials begun
Holding on to my beliefs
Raised nine children without too much grief
Through God and mothers love this was done
Gladly I start each day with fun
This I dedicate to my mom
She showed me how to dance and run
All my love, forever young

Florence Riddick
Barker, NY

Nantucket Dawn

Silence and sun that early morning
Between Jared's house and the wharves
Where I felt a palpable peace
With no one selling or buying,
I found at dawn only an uncertain sun
Dappling worn, uneven cobblestones.
The mute spirits of old, veteran whalers
Were there walking ahead of me or with me
Upon those same bricks, all around me they were.

Then to the harbor and to the straight wharf
I found still more silence save for a gull
Calling to me and to them, his sailor companions;
All the shops and those who ran them
Became simply a backdrop for this fabled town.
Those old sailors standing there with me in spirit
Would have liked some voices
At least a few words of compassion for the past,
But none came. Not a word. Then or now.

As I stood there with a heavy mist emerging
I thought of you, men of Essex.
I had read that many there were come to see you
And to count those who had returned.
You see, all the island had heard about your journey,
But on that day of return no words were spoke,
Neither compassion nor confession;
You who came back lived lives of aloneness
Among suspicious islanders on the streets of home.

Donald R. Eldred
Jacksonville, IL

*I return to the island whenever I can. This poem came to me almost fully put
together. I see and hear these spiritual old sailors who were with the Essex decades
ago and lost at sea for two years.*

A Real Winner

Lately I have been spending too much time
Thinking up words that actually rhyme
Hoping my poem is good enough to win
A sizable check to show all my kin.

If I win enough money, I would take my best friend
To a nice restaurant and start a new trend —
We'd be dressed in our finest and have lots of fun
Eating our fine dinner and sharing the last bun.

So, here's to dreaming of being a big winner
And enjoying some laughs with my pal over dinner,
But my social security check will pay for this one
As I am truly blessed after all is said and done.

I forgot to mention we had asked for the kids menu
They told us we were too old to get that venue.
"But, I'm in my second childhood, doesn't that count?"
The polite server had no idea what that was about.

Now that I think about winning a prize
It's not as important as seeing the sunrise.
My best friend and I can have fun doing nothing
And with the Lord guiding us — that is worth something.

Betty J. Staley
Sun City, AZ

I Forgive You

I forgive you for the broken promises
I forgive you for the shattered dreams
I forgive you for breaking my heart
I forgive you for damaging my self-esteem
I trusted you, I believed in you
I gave you my heart to protect it,
you gave it back to me in pieces
the protector, the confidant, the friend like
a switch you turned out to be my adversary,
my betrayer, my arch enemy
I forgive you for not being apologetic,
so is your love generic
I forgive you for holding me down
I forgive you for walking away like trouble
it only lasts a day
I forgive you for the pain,
and the love you never gained
I loved you with my whole heart and I always will

Connie Eiland
Birmingham, AL

The Impact

(On finding out I had stage III breast cancer)

How can you describe
The feelings deep inside
That stir within your soul?
To the deepest dark reaches
This illness does teach us
That you don't need two breasts to be whole

An "about face" in life
Is caused by this strife
The fear is nothing you've known
At my Lord's feet I laid
My burden, and prayed
That it wasn't my time to go home

There's too much to do
My life can't be through
My children need me alive
I'll do what I must
The hell with my bust
I'll fight the good fight to survive

And the sickness and pain
In his lap my head lain
My comfort was found in thee
My doctors he picked
And this cancer we licked
Thank you, Jesus, I'm now cancer-free

Tracey Travis Lee
Landenberg, PA

"Coke in a Bottle"

Summer of '69 cut off jeans Beatles tee and dirt roads
Girl stuff growing pains it's not all fairy tales and toads

Hours filled with penny candy "Coke in a bottle"

Too simple small town streets no ebbs no flow
Hope is beautiful it doesn't care who you know

Days filled with penny candy "Coke in a bottle"

Body innocent yet someday I fear there will be endless dues
Stars at night my only company as I share the daily clues

Years filled with penny candy "Coke in a bottle"

Dreams silent muted masked no one here soars
Not waiting to mirror anyone's life hear me roar

Life filled with penny candy "Coke in a bottle"

Kay Jo Collins
Modesto, CA

Return to Wonder

If you're questioning where the day just went
Or why your pace... so slow?
It's time to stop and wonder!
Time to watch your garden grow.

A garden is a miracle of
Life and death
Growth, re-growth, His power
Glorious beauty—along path, in bower!

It doesn't measure marigolds in minutes
Doesn't offer vibrant color by the pound
Rewards its owners in fireflies
As life goes 'round and 'round!

You have been a treasure in life's garden
To so many along your path,
Now it's time for joy and wonder
A resting spot... at last.

Caryl Van Alstyne Shugars
Crossville, TN

Thanksgiving Thanks

Let us bow our heads and express how we feel
As we gather together for our Thanksgiving meal
With family and friends that we will gladly share
Such a happy feeling for those that will be there
May we take time to look back on another year
Enjoying the time with all the ones we hold dear
Hopefully may we grow in our wisdom and love
Take time to celebrate and enjoy gifts from above
Now pass the turkey, dressing and gravy please
Then I will have noodles, cranberries and peas
Don't offer me any seconds I might say oh my
For dessert I think I'll have some coffee and pie
After everyone has eaten and all is said and done
Just turn on the TV for football games have begun
Let us bow our heads and express how we feel
As we gather together for our Thanksgiving meal

Dorothy E. Kissman
Austin, TX

I, Dorothy, was one of twelve children and blessed by having a great mother and father who both loved to cook and entertain—holidays were always special and we welcomed our relatives to join in. It was catch up time on who was doing what. Later TV became the topic of conversation and mostly the men enjoyed the football games—so TV became the source of entertainment. Before that, those were the good old days, but we still catch up on what is going on as we watch the TV and enjoy the good foods.

If I Didn't Have Jesus to Lean On

If I didn't have Jesus to lean on
As I travel life's uncertain road
When my steps are unsure and I trip on a stone
He catches me and carries my load

Yes, you've carried my load a number of times Lord
Why I guess it's been most of my life
But it's not me I'm asking this blessing
It's for my sweet lovely wife

She looked so still and pale lying there
After being under the knife
And I know you didn't bring us together
For a few short years
Just to take her life

So God, I'm asking for your healing touch
On the one I care so much for
I've never known a love so strong
But then you brought us to where we are

And if I didn't have Jesus I couldn't go on
My load is too heavy to bear
When the tears start to flow
And I can't see to go
I call Him and He's always there

Aron Wooten
Hooks, TX

Thanks Joe Billott

Joe, we want to wish you a very happy retirement
We hope for you and your family it's time well spent
We hope much new music you can now undertake
So much wonderful published music you will make
It has been a real pleasure to get to know you, Joe
As you given us many a laugh as your face did glow
You have always done your job with a lot of pride
A large wide smile on your face did so often reside
Joe, you have given us all a great deal of pleasure
And your time spent with each of us we will treasure
As the time we spent with you often made you smile
As you always wanted each one to stay a longer while
For each of us can say you gave us a whole lot of fun
We're all sorry your course of time with us has now run
Down South we hope you all will enjoy your new home
We hope it gives you much area in which you can roam
We wish you and all your family have the very, very best
Of times as you deserve a welcome nice long time to rest
You are surely someone that we won't very easily forget
For each and every one of us it's a pleasure we you met
We hope you enjoy the time with your family you spend
Which means on you for more things they can now depend
Well it seems that right now is the very appropriate time
To put a quick little end to "Thanks, Joe Billott" rhyme

Robert C. Magill
Pittsburgh, PA

I was born at West Penn Hospital on March 13, 1952. I have a BS in accounting from Duquesne University. I have been retired since July of 2011 after being employed in health care reimbursement auditing for almost thirty-five years by the Pennsylvania Department of Public Welfare. I am single and enjoy dining out, all types of soft music, dancing, gardening, spectator sports and genealogy.

Freedom

F   Freedom is not free, it comes with great sacrifices, as we all know.

R   Remember the price that was paid for our freedom, Christ died for us all. Now men and women are still dying to defend our God given freedom.

E   Enduring the suffering are the innocent men, women, and children.

E   Efforts are made for peace in the world, but still wars continue.

D   Don't despair or fear for God is always near.

O   Open your hearts to God's laws (Ten Commandments), then there will be freedom and peace all over the world.

M   May all of us work toward world peace through our allegiances to God and our country. *Then God will bless America!*

Joan Trombley
Bay City, MI

It's All About Time

Time, Time, how do we measure you
We divide you in half call you day and night
Divide you some more into seconds and minutes
That we mark on a clock listening to you tick and tock
We name you by seasons winter, spring, summer and fall
Time, Time, how do we save you
With machines that grind and roar and whistle
That rumble and groan and purr like a kitten
Time, Time, why do we need you
Regret you, anticipate you
You are like an alien burrowed into our minds
We think we can outrace you, evade you
Shackle you to our desires
Time, Time, you are the first thing we see
When we look into the mirror
For in our flesh you etch a design
Time, Time, you would be a friend
If only we could throw off that which binds us
The strident alarm, the time clocks to punch
The appointments we keep from dawn to dusk
If only for once we could call you nothing
We would have plenty of you, we would not feel rushed
But without you we would not exist
For you Time, are our lives, you are all we have
And seldom if ever are you enough, precious Time

Laura L. Paulsen
St. Paul, MN

Jesus You're the Best Thing That's Happened to Me

My life was a wreck, no future could I see:
Then, one night, I found Jesus, or Jesus found me.
He gave me hope, He gave me Faith, He set my spirit free.
Oh! Jesus, you're the best thing that's happened to me.

Oh! Jesus, you're the best thing that's happened to me,
My sin's all behind me, since you have set me free.
I have something now in which I do believe.
Oh! Jesus, you're the best thing that's happened to me.

These tears in my eyes are, now, for joy
At the mention of His name, my heart leaps with glee;
For, I know as I get older, in Him I'll grow bolder.
Oh! Jesus, you're the best thing that's happened to me.

This world holds nothing, but pain and misery,
Since I have found Jesus, it's so plain to see
All it's great riches or the fame that used to be.
Oh! Jesus, you're the best thing that's happened to me.

Timothy Dinkins
Melissa, TX

Angels Walk Among Us

Angels live forever
Far beyond our days on earth,
And every soul receives
A guardian angel at birth.

Invisible, these angels
Never leave us day or night.
They know our fears and whisper,
"Things are going to be all right."

They give us strength and purpose,
Keep our hope and courage strong,
They fill our minds with wisdom
And our spirits with a song.

They give hope when there seems none
Help believe you have courage within your soul
Filling you with strength and determination
And helping you finally become "whole."

When it is your time to leave
Their wings wrap around you tight.
And carry your soul to Heaven
Where everything is happy and bright.

Roxanne Patrice Bastian
Saskatoon, SK

Independence Day

Independence is so very pure and precious to each of us,
it must be earned and demands commitment and sacrifice,
and nothing less than respect and self-reliance advise.

We should care working 365 days of the year every year,
helping our country free itself from foreign involvement,
in justice, liberty, freedom and preservation of intent.

Yes, the United States of America, no more powerful words
ever written or said, a nation born of revolution framed
and formed by our founding loving fathers who reigned.

It was July 4th, 1776, that we claimed our independence
from Britain and on that day, democracy was finally born.
US is truly a diverse nation of dynamic people adorn.

The freedom that is inherent in the Stars and the Stripes,
our revered flag… celebrate freedom this holiday.
Land of the free, home of the brave and doing it our way.

Each year we celebrate as Americans on the 4th of July
freedom and independence with picnics, barbecues and more,
families gather enjoying friendship and fireworks galore.

First anniversary of the Declaration of Independence
was in Philadelphia, Pennsylvania, on July 4th, 1777,
bell ringing, cannonades and fireworks to high heaven.

Always remember our forefathers and what they had done.
Freedom, liberty and justice will prevail loud and clear,
as the American symbol of independence year after year.

Larry L. Schroll
Spring Grove, PA

Since my retirement, I find writing poetry fulfills my life to another degree, with special feelings of satisfaction and looking forward to another day in a very different way. I feel so honored that this poem has been recognized! Thanks Eber & Wein Publishing. This is such an incentive to keep on writing!

Life

What is the meaning of life?
It means different things to different people.
To some it means everything and to others it means nothing.
People who love life look forward to each day as a new day a new beginning, to others who know nothing but pain or mistreated by others find each new day is painful and unending.
Some of those who have never ending pain from being mistreated by others may choose to strike out at others even to the point of doing great harm to others.
Those of us who enjoy life look forward to sharing that joy with others.
They look forward to sharing that joy with that very special person.
Those of us who have hidden or built up pain are unsure how to deal with it.
They may find the joy for life again and heal or they may not and might try to end it.
If they find the joy of life once again the healing begins.
If they don't and they decide to end it, we all lose someone who could have been a great friend or soul mate.
In the end it is in the hands of God for he is the supreme being who has the power to forgive and to heal, for he is the father of us all.

Timothy H. Johnstone
Porterville, CA

Ah! Summer Is Here Again

Watching free floating clouds
Wipes away my fear and doubt
Across the clear blue sparkling sky
With birds flying joyously so high
Enjoying fragrance of blooming rose
And absorbing in the beauty's pose
With twinkling moon and lovely stars
Emitting light from near and far
Listening to the smooth flowing river
With shimmering and graceful cover
Where blissful nature is at display
Proudly filling with pure light's array
Now summer breeze is blowing again
Taking away tears of distress and pain
Bringing freshness and a life of delight
With beautiful smiles and splendid light
Ah! See again super summer is here
With magical colors of hope my dear
As it spreads joy and its cool breeze
And breathe new life of care and ease
Where cloudless and clear sky's part
Display Nature's magical and new art
And once again transforms hope bright
Into sunshine and brilliant summer delight.

Seema Chowdhury
Maple, ON

Leaving Cuba

"Vamonos, we must leave."
I wanted to stay
and play with my doll,
the only toy we owned.
My mother only repeated,
"Vamonos."
She lied and said it would
be a vacation, but a vacation
we would never return from.
I would never see my tía Lourdes
again or meet my cousin, Joaquín.
I would never see my friends
from school again, especially Miguel.
My mother told me he had
decided to stay with his abuelita,
but later on I found out the truth,
he had been eaten by a shark
trying to escape.
I couldn't bring my familiar clothes,
I couldn't bring my illegal books,
I couldn't even bring my only doll.
She stayed behind in an abandoned home
full of deserted dreams, oppressed hope,
and crushed faith.
I hated my mother for a long time,
until one day I realized — she saved my life.

Lisa Marie Perez
Moonachie, NJ

Where Are You?

Did you forget about me?
I am scared, I am unsure, I don't understand,
did you forget about me?
I don't want to go through this trial,
I don't know where it leads,
I don't know what's on the other side, are you there with me?
Walking next to me and pulling me through the bad parts,
closer to the end?
Too many questions I have,
too many dark corners I face,
everything is scary for me,
God where are you?
I need to climb upon your lap, and you tell me it's okay, that you
    won't leave me or forsake me, I feel helpless, God where are you?
I need your healing hand, your soft voice, a whisper of hope.
I need to find you again, to bring a soft warm light of hope
to my dark corners.
God will bring me peace for my soul,
rest for my questions, I will be silent and wait.
God where am I?

Barbara J. Valente
Redwood Valley, CA

*I wrote this poem when I found out my husband had cancer. I was so scared and
frightened. Cancer is such a scary word. God brought us through and now my
husband of forty-three years is cancer free.*

Deception

Feathers glisten like freshly fallen snow.
A golden halo resides above her head.
With the voice like a delightful symphony,
She is innocent and untouched,
A temptation for any with no will.
Dark, torn, and fallen, he stares.
Wings shredded and foul.
His deep desire for her consumes him.
He woos her relentlessly,
Desperate to gain her trust.
But she is cautious, protective of her heart.
A millennium passes.
And she has fallen in love.
With her heart open and revealed,
She is vulnerable to his attack.
He is deceitful and steals her glow.
She watches as her beloved flies away.
His ebony wings slowly begin to shine.
Her body weakens and her feathers darken.
Hair once platinum blonde, now chestnut brown.
She lies on her back in the dust.
She is defeated.
But still her mouth curves into a smile.
For she knows,
The devil can only stay an angel for so long.

Brandi Dunlap
Cheyenne, WY

The Ache of Loneliness

You are not necessarily lonely
when you are alone.
Many things can be accomplished,
talking on a telephone,
or even looking for something to demolish.

The ache of loneliness
can occur in a crowded room,
or when alone.
It feels like a dagger
piercing your heart.
It's a cloud
hanging over your head,
a symbol of gloom.

It's not depression,
nor can it be controlled
by suppression.
It cannot be faked.
It is daunting,
a haunting
ache of loneliness
reverberating in
the echoes
of your bones.

Tony Tripodi
Jacksonville, FL

My One True Love

For you my heart aches.
You are what love makes.
I've got what it takes.
My soul next to yours.
Neither of us keep scores.
My loving heart soars.
You are my love and all.
I'll catch you should you fall.
Our love will grow tall.

From our first gaze I fell in love.
You and I fit like a glove.
I fly high on your love as does a dove.
My love cannot be expressed.
No words enough stressed.
My Lord we are blessed.

For you are my true love won.
You and I have the best of fun.
I will always call you hun.
My body and soul long for you.
Nothing can stop us two.
Making love to you is what I want to do.
Your face and body is the ultimate beauty.
I'll fall for you, it's my duty.
Our love is an eternity.

Dan Forte
Burlington, ON

*I wrote this poem for the one I love who continues to inspire me
and fills my heart with love and joy.*

Don't You Wish?

Do you ever wish you could tell people what you really think?
Will we ever get government officials who actually don't stink?
Wish you could play bumper cars with bad drivers on the road?
Or smack certain people around without being punished for
    being bold?
Don't you wish you could snap your fingers and make things go
    your way?
Or magically rearrange your life when everything seems
    in disarray?
Would you like the opportunity to take justice in your own hands?
Restart anew when all else fails, even with all the best laid plans?
What about having to push twelve buttons to get through to
    customer service?
After waiting thirty minutes, you get transferred to someone who
    can't even speak English?
Do you ever get frustrated when solicitors ignore the sign on your
    front door?
Or do you want to punish the rich for getting richer while the rest
    of us just stay poor?
Do you wish you could take money from people who have more
    than they can handle?
Or control the media and newspapers in order to print real news
    instead of celebrity scandals?
Do you wish you could refuse and boycott right at the pump to
    lower the price of gas?
Or permanently remove the ceiling placed between upper, lower
    and middle class?
Don't you wish you could have the opportunity to relive your
    youthful years?
What about having big enough guts to successfully conquer any
    and all of your fears?
Or jump forward and backward in time to apply your wisdom to
    your youth?
What about having the ability to distinguish between embellished
    lies and the simple truth?

Julie Belisle
Windsor, ON

Embrace Life

Life, as precious as jewels,
process mature living,
today along your way,
embrace what's been given,
thank you to say,
means much to hear to one so dear.

Love, forever is eternal,
such joy one be given,
look and see all around,
as His love abounds.

Moments, but a flash,
yesteryear never again,
living through the chapters of life,
today cherish forever,
as tomorrow reflects joy given,
today.

Janice Richardson Hull
Peru, IN

The Life of a Soldier in a Faraway Land

He sadly says his final good-byes to his loved ones and off to war he goes, for this is the life of a soldier in a faraway land.

He fights for our country, our freedom as well. God bless our soldiers and our red, white and blue.

He's on his watch twenty-four-seven for he knows there's no time to waste for he was sworn to protect you and me even though he knows it might cost him his life.

He acts like tough disciplined warrior yet he's so gentle and sweet God protect our soldiers and always keep them safe.

In the still of the night when he's feeling homesick, lonesome and blue he'll pull out a picture of someone dear to his heart. He looks at the picture and then he holds it close to his heart that's when you see the tears come to his eyes.

He tries not to show it, his face he does hide, for he doesn't want his fellow soldiers to see that he cries.

He picks himself up and does his job well for that's what he was sent there to do. Sometimes, if there's a chance, he will kneel down and he'll say a small prayer.

Please dear God, my family I trust in your hands always keep them safe for me for I am far away doing the best that I can.

For this is the life of a soldier in a faraway land.

God bless America!

Mollie G. Salazar
Gallup, NM

My name is Mollie G. Salazar and with great pride, I would like to dedicate this poem to all our men and women in our armed forces. I would also like to say thank you to all our veterans who graciously gave of their time to serve this great country of ours. Although some of our brave men and women never returned home, they will always be remembered in our thoughts and in our prayers. God bless! I hope you enjoy reading this poem as much as I enjoyed writing it.

Hello? Is Anyone Awake?

This is no misty-eyed diatribe of lost days
that are slipping past.
Rather, it's a look from another angle
that came to me at last.
Our youth is spent wishing for age and responsibility.
Our adulthood lived so quickly, it flies by too busily.
Interwoven within the ages is what we truly crave:
freedom from the boredom that consumes,
occupying each age.
Some lives are crazy busy
and some are waiting to begin.
Either way, the boredom's at the fringes
ever present squeezing in.
How many live their lives jam-packed full
of routine tasks?
While giving little notice to their restlessness;
not searching deep enough to ask.
Freedom is often spoken of
in relation to liberation from dark times.
Yet how dark becomes the boredom of routine
that governs so many in their lives?
The answer to the boredom is greater
than can be found upon the planet.
Fore it is not until we've lived our lives through
that the answer is then granted.

Katie Penwell
Yellow Spring, WV

The World

The world is changing
The earth is giving way
The weather is changing
The attitude of the people is changing
The planes are crashing
The trains are wrecking
The food is changing
The way we eat is changing
The food is changing not for the good
The animals are being hunted
The world history is changing
The most beautiful living thing
The most beautiful people are being hateful
The teachers are speaking out
The teachers are being bad
The teachers are committing crimes
The teachers are getting away with it
The world needs to become a better place
Stop catering to the bad
Only support the good

Gladys L. Houser
Columbus, OH

It's Raining Animals

It's raining very hard, and yet, no dogs or cats I see.
It's raining other animals; they're falling over me.
It's pouring purple emus, dotted pandas—chickens, too,
And also cranky rhinos, and a crocodile or few.

A group of desert camels, toting parasols that gleam,
Are descending altogether in a fast, cascading stream.
It's raining wild horses, and bunny rabbits all a-hop,
And double-jointed giraffes with necks that never stop.

One hundred grumpy turtles, who're demanding to be fed,
Are falling very quickly. One just landed on his head.
It's raining leap frogs and crabs with shells so new.
I see a cheetah dashing in a streak of flashy blue.

It's raining regal puffins, also robins, worms in bill,
A school of fishes practices a collective diving drill.
A slew of madcap monkeys, full of gaiety and mirth,
Throw handfuls of confetti as they irrigate the earth.

It's raining hefty hippos; one is blowing a mean horn.
Look at the dandy lion with his mane so neatly shorn.
Here comes a lake of llamas in a saturating queue.
¡Dios mio, estan bailando on their wet trek from Peru!

Some mynahs are drizzling. They're falling in a swarm,
Swilling teacups of oolong as they prattle up a storm.
Kangaroos are now misting; joeys in their pouches tucked.
Since the clouds are clearing, the deluge will let up.

The rain is now subsiding—coming to an abrupt end.
I can hardly wait until I see the animals rain again.

Yvonne B. Arroyo
Vacaville, CA

*As a retired bilingual teacher, I continue to write rhymes for young second
language learners. I also love the Spanish language and seize every opportunity
to improve my knowledge of it.*

This Is Your Life

Lights flickering and spinning, like a film wheel
Turning, cycling 'round and 'round.
A young dark haired female
Walking down a sidewalk,
Blue crystal sky above with white clouds drifting,
While the soft gentle breeze greets her smiling face.
Beside her stand two elderly women,
Who smile and greet the comfort of the wind.
They each take the hand of the young one,
Walking down the nicely paved sidewalk.
Slight flickering, blinding light flashes onto the wall.
Trees, lakes, blue sky and an open road:
Everything perfect and content.
Only for disaster to show its face.
Shattered glass, broken metal flung to the side,
Sound of ear-shattering crunches and snaps.
As soon as it came, the light, the image fades,
Bringing back darkness into the room,
Spreading a feeling of hopelessness and fear,
Wishing to live again.
Tracing a door made with soft white light,
Creaking as it opens,
And to feel a hand on my chest;
Hearing someone say…
This is not a second chance at life… This is your life.

Tara-Lynn Courtepatte
Edmonton, AB

This has been a year of rebirth for me. In the week of Valentine's Day, my grandmother passed on from a stroke and joined my beloved best friend and older sister and paternal grandmother. Life and fate have a way of testing our limits. In the first week of July, my dear friend and I were victims of a rollover. We were pulled from the car into the arms of strangers. We were said to be lucky, but my angels were looking out for us to live the lives that we were born into.

Over the Rainbow

Sometimes you try too hard
To block the pain
You hold back so many tears
And then can't stop the rain
The storm just creeps up
Everything turning darker shades
Twisters forming in corners
Where you swore you felt no pain
Even in the darkest shadows
Under that bone crushing weight
You can't ignore that instinct
The need to look both ways

It takes a special kind of spark
To make lightning in this state
A certain angle to make that shine
Like the sun, on a cloudy day
Those eyes that can always see
The pain… behind the smile you fake
That person becomes your sandy beach
Your sanctuary, your set sails
Sifting through your cloudy head
To show you a place
The way to find your happiness
The key that makes your heart race

Hannah Brace
Millet, AB

The Creator's Page

Picture the beauty of our land...
Thank our Father for his work at hand.
We might have time to stop all the crazy,
First, we must stop developing the lazy.

The plush trees and their sucklings,
Destroy them all, along with the ducklings.
Everything will be extinct and no one left to lie.
All things will end because everyone will die.

The spring no longer will bring anew,
The true reality is very blue.
From babies, pups, grass and crops,
They will be no parents, moms or pops.

The seasons are just the murderers' starts,
It seems life forms just have no heart.
Builders, hunters, killers and flood,
Beauty turns to evil and all bask in devils blood.

God gave us everything but we cannot be pleased,
We try to defy the odds, while gratifying self-peace.
Bothering other worlds, to extending our old age,
High tech life as we know it, will erase our creator's page.

Sandra Jacobson
Carbon, AB

Being a writer for over thirty years and published over fifteen times, I still enjoy the freedom of entering my fantasy worlds to escape the "what is" reality. It's also a great way to help world issues or at least try to express what I see. I look forward to seeing my novel come to print, where more of the world's problems will be brought to light and hopefully bring great change.

Joel: In Memory Of

Soon after your mom and I wed you and I began to spend a lot of time together. Sometimes you'd accompany me to the laundromat where we chatted while doing laundry. Other times I'd help you with homework or you'd keep to yourself and read. The best times were when you'd confide in me expressing your feelings about school and how you felt that you were not like other kids your age. I felt you were sort of a loner among your peers, and at times withdrawn. As time passed, I discovered a tender hearted and compassionate son you were. There were times I wanted to call you my son, but didn't. I was hesitant to do so in fear you'd feel "rushed," as it were. Sometime later you left with your sisters and older brother for Jonestown, Guyana. Later on after your mom arrived in Jonestown, I got word that you "found yourself," were full of life and learning, and most of all, loved sailing on the Marceline.

Sometime later tragedy struck! Almost a thousand men, woman and children were murdered in mass, including you, your mom and sisters. Your older brother was in the capital city with other Temple members when the tragedy occurred. I lost you, my son, however gained another—your brother John. I call him son, and he calls me "Pops"... this in remembrance of you Joel, my son forevermore.

Guy B. Young
Grants Pass, OR

The River of Life

There's a river that flows
Past the hills and plains,
On to the ocean wide.

There are rapids and falls
And boulders in the way,
Along the river of life.

You may stop for awhile
And explore a great scene,
Finding renewal there.

You must venture back
To your boat and your route,
In spite of worries and fears.

There are storms and winds
And you can't find your way,
So you say, "I can't go on."

Keep your hand on the rudder
Hold firm to your course,
And keep your mind on God.

Ronald C. Kern
Floyds Knobs, IN

Love It

My mighty God is on my side, passion
of love that part of me I will never
hide, oh yes, I love it
Smiling a light that shines on my face
that part of me I will show in any case
oh yes, I love it
Walk the walk, then talk the talk, humbling
words, that show you'll smart oh yes I
love it
Your body language bounce then slide,
tap of the feet that glide to pass by
oh yes I love it
The blink of an eye that drains with tears
sadness that, shows no fear
oh yes I love it
This day will never fade away, knowing
that love in me will stay, oh yes I love it
Color red, yellow, black and white this will
always be in plain sight, they will never
fade away, people of color, a part of God's
true light
oh yes, I love it
huge and kisses surround time and sound
saying I love you with no frown
oh yes, I love it, this poem from the heart
I listen to God's words, he will always hold
my hand, I began to write, just knowing
he's near, but not in plain sight
oh yes, I love it
without him I cannot do, the writing
of beautiful words from me to you
"Oh yes," I love it

Patricia A. Allen
Baltimore, MD

Distraught

The sun is slowly setting
And as I begin my walk home, I feel the rain
The rain always insists to follow me
But I don't mind
I hold out my umbrella to others
Letting it shelter people who need it more than I
I have felt the sun and its warmth
But it can't compare to the kindness the rain gives me
For the rain masks my tears
The tears that must be shed for the battle
The battle that was both won and lost
I have done such terrible things
Yet
I am always told that I did what was right
But the demons in my mind say otherwise
And at the end of the day
I feel like I am being used as the rope
In the tug-of-war between Heaven and Hell

Samantha Peters
Winkler, MB

The Electric Pencil

"A pencil cannot tell you, what you are to write.
I pick one up and look at it, in the middle of the night.
Then reach into, the deepest core of my mind.
There, by some sort of coincidence I find,
What my heart, is really saying.

"A pen is only a tool, that's filled with ink.
It cannot tell me, exactly what to think.
So many of my words, keep falling off the brink.
Where the edge of my material, starts fraying.

"What type am I, do I even see,
That they have a habit, of slipping away from me?
Though the day's not free,
Like climbing to the top, of an old dead tree.
Where it slips on clothes, then staying.

"An electric pencil, just like the pen,
Hasn't any function, even towards the end.
It has to be picked up, entirely by hand,
To put thoughts down to paper, like wind over land."

Caroljo Nagel
Kimball, NE

Ripple Effect

One tiny stone thrown into the pond,
Leaves multiple ripples that go far beyond.
Though dropped to the bottom in careless thought,
It's unaware of the effect it has brought.

Like the stone, we too have a ripple effect.
Words splash from our mouths will little intent,
Then wash ashore to unknown places,
Not knowing the thoughts they soon will face.

The person hurt, lashes out,
And unaware sends ripples about.
An insignificant, callous remark,
Has now changed a once good heart.

Trust is gone, replaced by hate,
Continued ripples don't hesitate.
Under the guise of being right,
Thoughtless acts now lead to fights.

What if instead, words said are kind,
And the ripples spread to changing minds,
With acts of love that understand and
Show belief in each woman and man?

Would you choose to be a part,
To give the world a kinder heart?

Nancy Lauzon
Salem, WI

Before You Ask

Before you ask,
it seems as if this broken glass
has me in a death grip,
like you to my heart.
But I'm one to leave,
to care more and then not.
Before you look out the car window,
I've spelt it wrong again.
I should stand and close my eyes,
listen to the language of love
which is really your voice,
and try to reply in words I
can't seem to muster.
Before you wait any longer, stop.
And yet, I can't seem to let you go,
I smile when I do this,
when I've sunken to this point.
I just want you to hold me,
but I'd rather you not love me,
before you ask for too much.

Eman Akhtar
Ypsilanti, MI

For a Good Life

Keep on lovin'
Keep on learnin'
Keep on listenin'
Keep on readin'
Keep on smilin'
Keep on thankin'
Keep on acceptin'
Keep on givin'
Keep on forgivin'
Keep on appreciatin'
Keep on praisin'
Keep on seein' beauty
Keep on lookin' for good
Keep on enjoyin'
Keep on simplifyin'
Keep on dreamin'
Keep on workin'
Keep on havin' fun
Keep on deep breathin'
Keep on walkin'
Keep on stayin' beautiful
Keep on prayin'
Keep on havin' quiet time
Keep on bein' content
Keep on drinkin' cocoa

Bev Cull
Pewaukee, WI

Command and Condemned

I walk up to the gate of my past
Peering through the looking glass
I see myself shining bright
Feeling wise and full of might
I dance and sparkle in the moonlight
Twist and turn to the winds of life
But alas, the dance must stop
The sparkle must cease
The clouds are rolling in on this fragile me
I look to the dark clouds overlooking my soul
Hang on tight
Get a grip
This comes quick
Catch a glimpse
I'm not a dancer full of wisdom and might
I'm a puppet of lackluster
Strung tight, created to command
I struggle and pull and make my way to the looking glass
And what do I see?
My demented puppet master laughing at me

Racquel Antoinette Karson
Olmsted Falls, OH

Forgiveness Is Real

This morning the sun is rising high in the sky,
    Spreading sunbeams far and wide.

Last night's moonbeams have gone to rest.
    Oh, but what a sad sight has been left at
    Charleston's Emanuel AME Church!

There God's people had gathered for Bible study
    And gladly welcomed a stranger to join them.

Sadly an evil spirit came along with the stranger,
    Who massacred nine of God's loved ones.

No riot occurred as the stranger had hoped to incur. Instead,
    The loved ones of the murdered chose to forgive the murderer.

What a wonderful example of following God's prayer
    When we ask Him to forgive our sins as we
    Forgive those who sin against us!

God made each of us for a special purpose. We have different
    Skin colors, but our hearts are the same.

There is only one Heaven, and when I get to the gate
    And see someone whose skin is different from mine,
    I certainly will go on in full of joy. What will you do?

God made and loves each of us and I ask you to
    Treat all as you would like to be treated.

Burnell Burns L. Wood
Sumter, SC

Dreams

As I sit and look up at the sky
I think of all the memories gone by
Times once had
And now afar
The only thing shimmering
Is a shining bright star
And from that moment
As I think ahead
Visions of the future dance in my head
Times to be had
New memories to be made
Focus on happiness
And let the rest fade…

Rhonda L. Moran
Ludington, MI

March of the Splay-Toed Wizzles

A pride of splay-toed wizzles went marching up the path.
It surprised the farmer so, he nearly tripped upon his snath.
Now, if I were that farmer-man, and of course, if he were me —
Why, I'd hang my scythe upon a limb, and suddenly — I'd flee!

Roger M. Clough
Los Alamos, NM

Golden Serenity

Golden serenity
(A drunkard's poem)
Cold crisp starry night
Small consolation against the hated plight.
Life lighten in a hand woven chair
Peaceful sensations far flung stares.

Dead music echoes memories song
A wanton life long since gone.
Lucidity seeps in without abate
Forced restitution no bliss to sedate.

Laid plans were so near at hand
Of mice there is no time of sand.
A temporary paradise is within my grasp
Golden serenity at the bottom of a glass.

Eduardo Flores
Laredo, TX

My Children… My Treasure

Silently I listen. Sounds of rolling waves, they clash
Upon sun-kissed grains of sand. They mimic
Embryo's heartbeat… Nine months of carried safety
Their nest must finally break. Traveling through time
My mind does journey sweet. Dim the brazen lights
On distant trodden past. Embracing memories tight
Resonates deep. Within the shadows of babe's growth
Infant's skin so soft, flawless perfection. I long
To embrace. Kissing miniature digits, ten tiny toes
And fingers grasp. Begin to see life's future
Mother Earth is at their feet. Sparkling eyes so fresh
With truth and optimistic visions. Untainted yet
By jaded tribulation's sting. I watch. A mother sits
On sideline safe, to gently offer guidance. Careful
Not to smother. Neither of her budding roses' glory
Patience is a virtue must. But proud I am they bless me
I teach Truth's lessons proud and tall. One by one
Hope for grounded solace. Or does it ground me instead?
Proof presents itself as ever present. They've mastered
Daily I behold their grace and beauty. Reminding us
Destiny takes belief. Laughter, life's magical key
To harness energy bright. Ride their wings of progress
Birth… unfolding wonders pure in heart. Unconditional
Yet by their earthly birth, they birth our spirituality
My children… my treasure. Life's rarest jewel of all.

Bonnie S. Locke
Boca Raton, FL

Life: as a child it begins with imagination, and that teaches us to dream. Our visions grow simultaneously with us as time passes. We finally blossom into divine individual creativity. Yet only in seeing life through our own children's eyes do we fully grasp its meaning and purpose, for that is truly where life's creations take us… home. Thank you Alecia and Megan for being my children… my treasure, life's rarest jewel of all. I love you!

Farm Life

From the first rays of morning sunlight
As they peek over the distant hills,
Til the rays filter through the cracks
And the inside of the barn it fills.

The gentle rustling of the animals
The horses bump against the rails,
The barn doors squeak as they open
Here comes the farmer with his pails.

The sweet smell of the fresh hay
The sound made as he scoops the corn,
The slight clucking of the chickens
As he gathers the eggs each morn.

The sounds of farm life are relaxing
Sounds of nature, the animals and of man,
All is well in the morning's activities
I just wish he would stop and warm his hands!

Ron Terry
Andalusia, AL

Peace Triolet

There would never be war,
If the world were filled with love.
Only killing we would abhor,
There would never be war.
Every person we would adore,
Always praising God above.
There would never be war,
If the world were filled with love.

Joan Patterson Yeck
Moosic, PA

This poem is one of three poems about peace that I contributed to "The World's Largest Poem for Peace" at the United Nations. The senseless killing of innocent people is heartbreaking and we see so much of this in the news everyday. If everyone would treat other people with love and respect there would be no hatred or bloodshed and we could all live in peace and harmony. As Americans, God has given us so many wonderful blessings. We must all thank Him and pray for world peace! I love poetry! Thank you for letting me share it.

The Candle

A candle put inside a room
Surrounded by the darkness there and
It flickers on to clear the gloom.
A moth flies by as if on cue
Its erratic flight was nothing new.
This pattern draws it nearer still —
The shadows on the wall are real.

David H. Rembert Jr.
Columbia, SC

Towards the Skies

She lifts her eyes
Towards the skies
Around her are the butterflies
In her stomach, they also hide
For weeks and weeks they fluttered by
He's just not like the other guys
But she's fragile and just as shy
He's a constellation in disguise
She's like the anchor to which he's tied
So she lifts her eyes
Toward the skies
And whispers her good-byes.

Rachel Legiec
Fort Myers, FL

Collecting Dust

You were like my favorite book.
You were the story I kept coming back to
Over
And
Over.
Choosing you in the first place wasn't my mistake.
It was picking up the book
Again
And
Again
And somehow thinking that the ending would be different.
I've learned my lesson now.
Our story is staying on the shelf,
Doing nothing more than collecting dust.

Hannah Mann
Glendale, AZ

Dark Friend

I've begun to love your
Come and go
Sometimes calling to me, or not
Your careless to and fro
The bright days
Crashing to times where I
Feel so...
Tired
Can't sleep
From the wracking ebb and flow
Of tears
But part of me somehow has
Begun to grow
On you, though the
Cruel winds come knocking, their
Shifting blow
Always changing
Summer's breeze to
Winter's snow
Though now
After ten endless years, I know
I couldn't be
This person I've become
Without my
Shadow

Danielle J. Wallace
Rumney, NH

Silent Cries

I didn't ask to be born.
Yet, I am here.
My soul tells me it's a
scary place, Yet, I feel happy.
I tell my soul you are wrong.
Souls are never wrong.
I see different faces coming
and going all the time.
My soul is worried. I am too.
Then one day it happens.
I am hit and hit.
My soul is crying, crying and crying.
My souls asks what did I do wrong.
I am a child, I do right and wrong
things, that's what a child does.
Yet, I am hit, I see their faces,
they are happy, laughing while
they hit me like a punching bag.
Finally, I feel my brain turning
to mush.
My little body goes limp. I am dead!
My soul screams out loud, I
didn't ask to be born.

Anabel Cuellar
Falfurrias, TX

Treasured Moments

Secret places,
    treasured moments,
      hidden,
        not completely lost.
Take me there
    to visit often,
    lest I forget
      what truly counts.

Sr. Regina Fierman CSA
Broadview Heights, OH

Homeless Man

I am educated, intelligent, patient and kind.
I have lost confidence in myself and peace within me I cannot find.
I have nowhere to turn, no place to live.
I have no money for housing to give.
I am homeless, you see.
Please do not judge or laugh at me.
Help me! Help me! I know you can.
I need someone to pray for me because I am a homeless man.

Erasala B. Cody
Tuscaloosa, AL

Amen

You've shot a light in the dark
And you wonder if you've gone too far
But you're too dim to be a true shining star
I remember when we felt within
Every word and touch and sin
Back then, every day ended with "amen"
You've gone now, to your favorite store
Where they give a license to kill
In exchange for falling to the floor
You've been through the beds of many men
There's us, but how many came before then?
How many whispered to you, "Amen?"
You say I haven't given much
I don't even remember your touch
But if it's sin, then I'll treat it as such
But there's always a march of lovers when
A woman is weeping and
Everything they say is a blind "amen"
It's all too familiar, dear
Just as empty and just as clear
Just as it was when I lived here
I know what you'd say, my friend:
"It will be like this again and again
Until you've found your own perfect amen"

William Duncker
Corpus Christi, TX

When Dusk Rises

It attacks like a winter breeze,
sneaking between cracks
of a misbuttoned sweater,
melting my cheeks in the cozy cavity
of the lonely iris I call home.

And I am lost.

The water dances around bare breasts,
and we swallow the lake.
It drowns in our bodies,
fish flapping against our tummies
begging for a freedom we seemed to have.

And the night took a picture of it,
our skin swarming the dock
and with the wood became one,
and our breath became echoes,
carried through the shadows,
lost as the sunrise washed them away
like they never even happened.

And the photograph frozen in a time gone,
like Walt Disney's body preserved in ice.

But it's all a conspiracy theory anyway.

Amber Conroy
Kinnelon, NJ

Surprising Love

I've been so blessed these many years
that friendship found its way
intertwined into my life bringing
happy thoughts each day.

It didn't take a second or a
minute to occur but days through
weeks and many months flowing into years.

Slowly working magic wonder until that
very day of waking up, to know how rare
it gives in many ways.

From one who… takes time to lend a
listening ear or
smile just right when sad days appear or
has a very special laugh to bring
that happy tear.

Friendship is a present
a box to open up
echoing memories of those who
will always be…

Your loving friend.

Kathleen Cronk
Mesa, AZ

To all who have entered and touched my life in this way… thank you.

Don't Leave

This can't be real
No I can't feel, feel tonight
You left me alone
On my own, breaking inside

Tonight, I'm afraid that it's true
That you'll leave just like he said
That he's right, and nobody cares
You'll tell me I'm broken, and just leave me there
Please just stand by me, don't leave

All you hear
Is that you're a mistake, something is wrong
Not good enough, never will be
You don't belong

I just want someone to see me
Someone to understand
Maybe I'm not broken, and just know who I am

Tonight, I'm afraid that it's true
That you'll leave just like he said
That he's right, and nobody cares
You'll tell me I'm broken, and just leave me there
Please just stand by me, baby please just please don't leave

Amber Jakiel
Allendale, MI

The Illusion of Time

Our time has come to leave...
Our triumphs, thy memories
As we pass this burden down...
Please... remember our legacies

As what we know, comes to a close
And our uncertainty becomes well-known...
Please have mercy upon our souls...
Because it seems that our future...
Will be... drastically unknown

But then this darkness of uncertainty...
Is shattered... by a glimmer of hope
Rising our ashes of uncertainty...
In to the forge, of greatness

And thus...
Our spirits live on, with certainty...
To serve the rest of our lives, with...Time on our side
To better this world... for the rest of mankind

And even after, our bodies have vanished by Time
Our legacies live on...
In this:
"Illusion of Time"

Corey Lyn
Odessa, FL

Grateful

I'm grateful for mornings that God wakes me up,
I'm grateful to feel his loving touch.
It's summer again and the sky is beautiful and clear,
It lets us know that God is always near.
The trees are all green and the tulips are up,
And there's even some yellow buttercups.
I'm grateful to greet my neighbor as they pass by;
I have to say hello and sometimes I just say hi!
We must always be thankful for the blessings he sends our way,
And always remember it's best his way.
So many changes are happening today,
They're trying to take God's word out of the way,
All we can do is just kneel and pray.

Frances Earl
Chattanooga, TN

Evensong at Westminster

Forever lying in repose
Whilst future generations sing,
Their voices lifted up in praise
To Heaven's own exalted king.

Harmonies of celestial sound
In madrigals ethereal.
Should marble stone have ears to hear
A slumber quite imperial.

Kings and queens and philosophers
Take rest under visitors' gaze.
Remembered each and every one
In sacred songs of solemn praise.

Theresa Zweig
Pittsburgh, PA

La Dolce Vita

Take in the majesty of a nighttime sky
The stars that shine—twinkle from God's eye
Let them lead you to walk straight and true
And have a confidence in all that you do

May your life be filled with a fire, and its passion
But see beyond temptations from the gods in fashion
If things seem to happen without any good reason
Understand, and move on, like the changing seasons

See above all that you might find as tragic
Trust the strength of the spirit—for it is magic
Feel rhythm in your heart, with each step, every day
For the breath of the soul will guide your way

Seek simplicity, and precious moments to treasure
Know the laughter that comes with the smallest of pleasures
Never be wary of adventure and discovery
If you slip or fall—be sure of the recovery

May you find happiness, without sorrow and pain
Brilliant sunshine, and shelter from depressing rain
May you move gently, without anger or strife
To indulge yourself—with the sweet life

Jill D. Gerlach
Kingsport, TN

Own Thy Own

As it is said, to thy own self be true,
What you show is what people look up to.
Inside of you is what you possess,
It is a way, in which you express.
Everyone can see how genuine,
Because it clearly so, does define.
There's a saying that goes, you're true blue.
What you say, is what you do.
And what you are is what you attract,
But you know this as matter of fact.
Learning you can be truer than true,
Affects everything in which you do.
This in itself, makes you consistent.
You're no longer left in the distance.
Lost, been a sense of reality.
Gain, is a sense of totality.
So when you do speak, try to make sure,
Understand, your words can be the cure.
There will come a time, to own thy own.
Please, do not fear, you're never alone.
When you learn, to thy own self be true,
You also find, life becomes anew.
The truth is always, right there behind.
Truth is free, truth is kind, truth's not blind.
To own thy own, helps to set you free.
Realize, own thy own, is the key.

Lynette Mack
Cape Coral, FL

Wordsmith

A wordsmith.

A sculptor shapes wood, stone, and ice.

A painter blends colors.

A musician harmonizes sounds.

A scientist discovers.

A poet finds the write word,
At the write time,
In the write syntax,
To express the write feeling
To the write person to read it in the write way.

A master of language juxtaposition.

A wordsmith.

Saisa Neel
Annapolis, MD

Spring Magic

                                          Aeaeae

the quietus, through the vicissitude of seasons

                                          Aeaeae

the enthuse, through 'cessation of calumny

                                          Aeaeae

the imago, through solid vortex

                                          Aeaeae

the aposiopesis, through jactation of explosive color as if a show
   of profligacy

                                          Aeaeae

the anodyne, through ataraxia of gentle blossoms

                                          Aeaeae

the halcyon, through cacophony of feathered ones

                                          Aeaeae

the amatory, through nature's adjuration of salient efforts

                                          Aeaeae

the nullibiety, through confluence of sinuosity

                                          Aeaeae

the gibe, through the quibbling of bees and newly hatched eggs

                                          Aeaeae

the consecrate, through ineluctable exposure to sun
Aeaeae

Peta-Gaye Vernon
La Jolla, CA

Harder Days Make Stronger Knights

Every day we wake up is a blessing in disguise,
An opportunity to be more, to do more, and to just try.
To try to be better, to try to maintain,
And to try to move forward past all of the pain
From a life we've toiled for, and battles we've fought,
From the scars that we wear and all that we've wrought.
As knights of the realm between the dark and the light,
While keeping the balance, we must be ready to fight
For all that we love and all we hold dear,
Harnessing strength from all that we fear.
We see the challenge and dare not back down.
We set our feet, and *we* hold our ground.
And when *we* slide back, and perhaps even fall,
We get back up and will ourselves to stand tall.
To brace for the impact, be strong through the pain,
And to fight through the tears until we regain
Whatever ground we have lost, and dreams we can't see,
And whatever it was that we wanted to be.
Clutching at our calm that aches to flee like a bird,
While trying to focus through the mundane and absurd.
Reminding ourselves life gives us what we can bear,
"Many hands make light work," so some burdens we share.
'Til our bodies give out and our minds are no more,
When our last breath is taken, and our soul longs to soar
Towards the heavens on wings we forged in this life
In moments of love and of joy, and of sorrow and strife.

Joanne G. Gruettner
Downsville, NY

The Death of a Poet

It shall be the death of me
And I can only let it be,
Close enough to kill me now,
I hardly care to wonder how
I fell this far from poet's world
To dark abyss coldly hurled.
Not a single word of comfort,
A mute whose ears are also hurt,
The power is gone from my head,
Inkless pen, the language dead.
It died first, I followed after,
I no longer hear the laughter
That killed us both in cold blood
Took all we had right where we stood.
It doesn't matter what they say,
We cannot hear them anyway.

Sarah Henriquez
San Antonio, TX

I am a senior in high school from San Antonio, Texas. I am a poet, and I always have been. My worst flaw, and perhaps my greatest strength, is that I can do nothing dispassionately. Poetry is my chosen form of expression because so much can be said in so few words. I have had twelve poems previously published and I hope to publish an anthology soon. Through my poor words, I hope to remind those who see my work that they are not alone. Indeed, literature forbids anyone to live in isolationism. That is what has saved me. This is everything I have to show, please forgive me all my straw.

The Suck of Death

Purity life defines morality,
sinful decaying thoughts,
deteriorating human elements,
tradition degenerates inferior,
annuity resting within,
as death reigns precision,
darkness sleeps captive,
the enemy lurks dominion,
on and around your soul…

Leslie Tellez
Bolingbrook, IL

Time

Time is measured by the tick of the clock,
which should tell us all, to reflect and take stock.
Of what we have done with the time that has past,
because what time is left, will seem to go by too fast.
Time waits for no one as the old saying goes,
just like the water that runs along as it flows.
So treasure your family, as you look ahead with great pride,
because when it's all said and done, hopefully you enjoyed the ride.

Jerry Strinden
Rancho Cucamonga, CA

Writing poems has provided another opportunity for me to share my thoughts and also read other poems from a cross section of creative individuals.

Peaceful Sea

Summer breeze rolls through the outrageous green trees
no one is there no one is seen,
the sand blows up from the beach.
You can feel a cool breeze and all of summer's ease.
The water so cold to touch,
you want to go swimming so much,
you're the only one out there,
thinking if you should break the calmness of the sea
and go swimming.
I think of you and I change my mind
thinking another mood another time,
when peace isn't so beautiful,
that if it was broken you would feel terrible.
As I walk quietly back up the beach,
I hear the cars beep, I hear the cars screech.
As I wander on I will never forget,
the peace I let carry on, on the beach…

Theresa Bruno
Avenel, NJ

I started writing poetry and songs at the age of thirteen. With the help of my grandmother, I accomplished writing a thirty-six-page book of poetry that was completed in 1984. I own the copyright of the book named Exploring and Expressing Feelings of Love and Life. *It's in the Library of Congress. It's never been published. I never could afford publishing fees and did not want to pay to have my work published. I almost sold a few songs to Rainbow Record in 1985 but they wanted me to pay them to include the songs on an album. My grandmother warned me that it may be a scam, so I didn't do it.*

Summer Solstice

Once upon a childhood dream
The season of summer did gleam
The scent of magnolias, daffodils galore
Lovely lilacs and peonies full of allure
With forsythia and japonica emitting colure
The fresh smell of laundry blowing in the breeze
Honeysuckle blossoms and buds filling tall trees
Roses on the trellis so delicate — so fair
A sight to behold ever so rare
Marigolds, zinnias, nasturtiums of flare
All the flowers under Addie's tender care
The hum of the mower going 'round and 'round
For with Bob Evans nary a weed could be found
A tomato, an onion, a pepper or two
Our dad knew just what to do
The 4th of July brought such a sight
The backyard looked liked the northern lights
Sparklers glowing — spitting fire to our delight
As fireflies gracefully immersed in the night
Ghost tales whispered under the stars
My sister protecting me from the men of Mars
Jeep rides and a picnic or two
From these times my memories grew
Stored in my mind and heart
These blessings will never part

Ruth Angle
Huntingdon, PA

Final Conversation

Tonight's a night for walking
Lonely deserted streets "goodbye"

She said and there was that silence
No one knows how to break as

We stood there in the room
Face to face and hand in hand

Like the beginning of a quadrille
"Goodbye"—ah, the finality of it

The end of each syllable like
A bell tolling mass, reverberating

Into an implacable nothingness
How religion annoys me

Goodbye, she said and my body
Turned to salt, turned to sand

Turned to lead here where I stand

"I hope I see you again," she said
"You never know at my age"

Matthew Loeterman
Fair Oaks, CA

This poem was written after my final visit with my beautiful mother before her passing on. May she rest in peace.

Raindrops on a Tin Porch Roof

Lightning flashes in the distance,
the night sky lights up.
Soft growing thunder rolls across the hills.
Wind whispering through the trees
as leaves rustle helplessly.
Raindrops fall on a tin porch roof.
A few here and there,
then all at once, heavily.
Wind chime drowned out
from the roaring of the downpour.
Down... down... down...
the drops relentlessly fall.
The clamor on the tin porch roof... fills my ears.
Flash! The night sky lights up.
Thunder rolls, moving on.
The wind shifts.
The once roar of the rain,
now tipper taps on the tin.
Faint flashes and thunder in the distance...
far away now.
No movement, no wind. All is still.
A lone cricket chirps.
Into bed, cool covers, soft pillow.
Drowsy memory carries me away...
Lost in the fading recollection
of raindrops falling on a tin porch roof.

Dillen Anderson
Sunbright, TN

*This is a poetic moment captured in verse, as a late night thunderstorm
passes and I sit on the front porch with pen and paper.*

The Fairy Queen

I was in my flower garden one day
when I spotted a fairy queen.

She was perched on a toadstool
combing her golden hair.

She jumped down, and on her head
a sombrero she did wear.

In her hand she held a quirt,
and she wore a dazzling western shirt.

She wore tight blue britches
and cowboy boots with fancy stitches,
and shiny silver spurs.

She hopped aboard her butterfly,
touched him with the spurs
and away they flew.

My oh my, what a wonderful dream
about my beautiful fairy queen.

Wilda Downing
Marcola, OR

Goldenrod Endless

Goldenrod Endless... the Summer gave me You
My thoughts turn back
On this lonely stretch of road —
Goldenrod Endless... and it's late afternoon
As the curves embrace me the Sun goes down
Dragging the summer's blazing heat

New millennia... but here it's 1962 and Florida and
Goldenrod Endless... a fruit stand... shells... souvenirs...
Moccasins and self-serve honey
The Nature Coast giving its best gifts to me...
Bear Crossing — old sugar mill
The manatee frequency on the radio
Crossing the Suwannee dark as tea
Deep in gator and cypress knee

A moment's tenderness comes back to me... in the half light
Your face, your well-worn hands, your smile
Deer spring into the woods, a coyote runs across the road
Red-tailed hawk trails over a field of wild hog
Passing through the lower hammock
The smell of water from the springs... the air grows colder
Closer... I drop down through hanging cypress and rock
To hear the echoes of children as sun hits turquoise water
And it's August and I remember...
Goldenrod Endless... I'm coming back... devoted to You

Tommie Richardson
Lakeland, FL

Sometimes

Sometimes
We say the wrong things
without realizing that we hurt
The same
Sometimes
We forget
To encourage dreams
We both need to gain
Sometimes
We don't understand
We both do the best we can
Sometimes
We lose touch of feelings
We both share
Sometimes
We overlook the special bond
We created
Sometimes
We forget
I'm sorry mends the broken heart
Sometimes
We misunderstand
Life
The same

Shelli Anne Childson
Christmas Valley, OR

Brothers... Till

If ever there was a brother loved
Here on earth and in the hereafter
He was mine.
We shared memories, laughter and many good times.
When I think of him... it breaks my heart every time.
His life was cut short, but his memory lives in my heart.
I never dreamed that we would ever be apart.
I loved my brother, body and soul
That's why I still ask myself...
Why did he have to go?
I loved him so much and I miss him so.
We parted ways in life in a way I don't accept,
But he is in Heaven now and by God, he is blessed.
Though his life was short... I'll never forget,
He was the best brother yet!
We were close in life and he was always by my side,
Someday... again we'll meet on the other side.
I treasure our time together
And... I will forget him never,
His memories are alive in my heart forever.
If ever there was a brother loved
Here on earth and in the hereafter...
He was mine.
We shared memories, laughter and many good times.
When I think of him... it breaks my heart every time.

Hermelinda Simmons
Spicewood, TX

Froggie

Froggie, Froggie, sitting on a lily pad
Froggie, Froggie why so sad?
Everyday you jump and hop ever so high
Once I even saw you jump as high as the sky
Please tell me Froggie, beautiful and green
Did someone treat you mean?
No, it's not that at all you see
My pond is drying up, so I must flee
I hope to see you again my friend
Maybe there's a beautiful pond around the bend
Until we meet again, I bid you farewell…
Did I ever see Froggie again? I will not tell

Rebecca Roach
Altamonte Springs, FL

Thieves and Robbers

Thieves and robbers, I hear you cry, punches and blows
And big black eyes, what's happening in our society
Hatred and anger, no tranquility, violence vs. sanity
We have our wants, still need our needs!
There is a void among us now, fill in the gaps
We must learn how, we must learn now be able to see
We cannot function lacking unity, be kind to your
Brother on the sides of the road, by the seeds he's sown
He has a heavy load, he's all diseased, eaten up by
The plague, have love and forgiveness, but don't be
Vague! We love our brothers just as ourselves
If you have questions, we have the help
I know some things, you cannot steal, are the
Things that are honest and the things that are real
You can take all I have materially, but you
Can't take my thoughts of what I see
You could learn this yourself, a brand new start,
If you clean up your act and righten your heart
Don't take from your brother what you cannot give
He has a right to laugh and live, come up from
Your furrows and get out of you ruts! Quiet
Dealing in lying and cheating and smut!
It's a shame how you treat your neighbor,
And a shame how you treat yourself, the
Effort is not in the labor, but whether you
Hurt or help!

Linda J. Lieber
Greenville, CA

The inspiration for this poem flowed freely after I returned home one evening to find out that I had been substantially "ripped off" by "raiders" in the night! Being robbed leaves a big void feeling and as I was pondering on "why did this happen to me?" it occurred to me to count my blessings, that my daughter and I had not been home at the time of the theft!

What Is Love?

A longing, a desire, an obsession with something that makes your
heart burst,
Is this what defines love?
What is love?
A kind gesture, a warm smile, the comfort of an arm draped across
your shoulders,
Is it putting your life on the line to save those whom you do
not know?
Taking an extra shift because you want to take your family on the
vacation of a lifetime?
Is it a moment around the fire eating marshmallows and singing
out to the stars,
Dreaming about what lies ahead,
A kiss on the cheek,
The laughter of a child, or the song of a sparrow,
The melting of the sun behind the evening clouds, or the piercing
tip of cupid's arrow
What is love?
A soft hoot of an owl to calm late night nightmares,
The image of fairies still fresh in a toddler's mind,
Is love presents on Christmas or a rose on Valentine's Day?
A chocolate dipped berry or a jeweled pendant
Love is not something that can be given lightly,
It weighs one down like a burden,
Oftentimes it can cloud one's judgement
Love is a double-edged sword, it can have positive and
negative outcomes,
Love draws out jealousy, but it also welcomes compassion
What is love?
Love is kindness, hope, longing, a might
Love is what turns darkness back into light

Aleksandra Werner
Phoenix, AZ

In a Child's Eyes

In a child's eyes,
they see the world in a different light.
Where we see pain and sorrow,
they see someone to hug tight.
In a child's eyes,
they see chances to try again.
Never giving up
until they've reached the very end.
Everything is true.
Helping one another is
always the best thing to do.
In a child's eyes,
no one really goes away.
There's no pain and sorrow
when you'll see them again someday.
Simple things is all they see.
Doing things to keep the earth
and revive humanity.
In a child's eyes
there's no task that's too small.
If you put your mind to it,
they believe that you can do it all.
Could you imagine how wonderful the world would be?
If you could see the world as they see…
in a child's eyes.

Ruth Brabant
La Crosse, WI

Poetry is a wonderful way to get imaginative, creative, and just let your mind go.

I am

I am not wasted
I am simple and plain
I am girl
I am a woman
I am a mother
I am a whore
I am a conservative

I am shape
I am mirror
I am design
I am lines

Curving
Jagged
Fierce
Molten

They are hazel
The strands are gray
The locks are brown
The color is alabaster
The height is average
The build is indifferent

I am pulse
I am wonder
I am…

Veronica King
Nogal, NM

The Path to Be Trod

When you're walking in the shadow
Of beliefs that are not true,
Your vision blurs and trembles
While the sky's no longer blue.

Pre-born lives are ended,
Morals daily slashed,
While those who force these tenets
Are a breed whose values crashed.

Take heart! The path they've laid
Can be mercifully trod
When you hold within your hand
The map that leads to God.

He waits before your crossing
Of the bridge to deep despair
And will tell you not to tremble.
What you have to do is care.

Stand tall! Walk straight! Be fearless!
For then you will control
The mindless moral assaults
On the contents of your soul.

Ann Sheridan
Washington, DC

Although I've written television scripts, newspaper articles, essays on various subjects and political satire, what I enjoy most in the creative process is the challenge of conveying in rhymed and metered poetry an idea one feels is worth sharing. I was schooled when literature was taught in every grade and I became fascinated by the mathematical aspect of metering, particularly after discovering Gilbert and Sullivan operettas. Granted, blank verse, even in song lyrics, is more the style now but it cannot beat the "beat" of metering to get the listener's or reader's attention.

I Remember

How well I do remember
That beautiful December
When we went sliding in that marshmallow snow,
The time your cute snub nose
Turned white and almost froze.
It filled my beating heart with sudden woe.

Remember that day in May
When we nestled in the hay?
It was the first time that we kissed.
As I recall that glorious time
I think of it in romantic rhyme,
And I realize I much have missed.

How often I recall
Those moments in the fall
When we skipped through the kaleidoscopic leaves
And I kissed your luscious lips.
Recalling now, my heart does flips,
And my hungry mouth for yours sorely grieves.

Yes, my dear, I do remember
From September to September,
Even as the years go flying by.
Each night I ask our evening star,
Wondering where and how you are,
"Do you remember as do I?"

David Epstein
Albuquerque, NM

My Love

My love for you, has always been true
From the very time, I said I do
Through the good times, and the bad
All the laughs, and being sad
I have always loved you

Years have come and years have gone
Now a family to call our own
Ups and downs may come our way
But my love for you is here to stay

If we should say goodbye down here
I will meet you again in Heaven dear
For I will always love you

Judy Pannell Moon
Vinemont, AL

Unlucky

People always tell you
Life is what you make it
Then why is it the hardest working people
Get the short end of the stick?
Is the lower middle class unlucky?
Is luck passed down
From one generation to the next?
What is luck anyway?
Some mystical force that not enough
Of us pay our tributes too?
A shooting star? A dandelion?
A penny with one's birth year on it?
And why then does working hard not earn us
The wondrous ways of "luck"
If you ask me… and yes no one ever has
Luck is simply having the right devices
When opportunity comes knocking
We, of the lower middle class, often forget
We make our lives what they are
And we have the power
To change our own circumstance
Without the luxuries of "luck"

Cierra Merryman
Hampstead, MD

Confusing Compound Words

Did you ever consider how our words are amusing?
Or on the other hand, they can be quite confusing.
Do you park in your driveway and drive in the parkway?
Or think about walking in the walkway,
Yet models shouldn't run on the runway?
Do you do your school work at home
And your homework at school?
Boy, your friends must think I'm a crazy old fool.
And that delicious hamburger all sizzling and hot
Is not made of ham, no pork should be sought.
And then there's the pork-barrel no pig in that pot.
It's the extra additions of Congress, is it not?
Then you have bookends that aren't made of books.
Or having a watchdog, but it's a person who looks.
A peanut may pass for the size of two peas,
But a walnut, come on, there is no way.
Is it as large as a wall? No never, you'd say.
Do I make my point even though it's not sharp?
Do you get my drift though the sands do not part?
Am I a little off my rocker,
Although from a chair I did not fall?
Are our words amusing or just there to recall?
So our speech can be clever, thoughtful, and nice
Or full of ill-disposition and spice.
God loves us and cares for us a lifetime of days,
So let's use our words to be overflowing with praise.

Carolyn MacHose Steiner
Fairlawn, OH

My first published poem was "Ode to Golf" in Beyond the Sea: Rhapsody *(2015). This poem was inspired by my father, Robert Lawrence MacHose, who always wanted to write a song about confusing compound words, but he never did. This poem is dedicated to him.*

Oy-Vey, Oy-Vey

When you're feeling down and out
and nothing comes your way
cup your forehead in your hands
and say oy-vey, oy-vey

You could say holy-moly
or even ai-yai-yai
but nothing soothes like oy-vey, oy-vey
and I really don't know why

The world is going crazy
crazier day by day
cup your forehead in your hands
and say oy-vey, oy-vey

Don't let the blues get you
tomorrow is a brand new day
just cup your forehead in your hands
and say oy-vey, oy-vey

Howard C. Klein
Boca Raton, FL

And the Results Are

A woman sits across from me so pale,
halo shattered overhead, angels surround.
Her legs shake shamelessly for bail,
as she remembers all the "in bed" hounds.
I can't adjust my eyes from her face,
the mist of fear that pours down in depth.
She staggers back and forth at an awkward pace,
Truth from her eyes spelled the secret use of *meth*.

Ring tone from a cell interrupted a thought,
so reading material became a must.
Including time desperately needed to be bought,
to restart a life facing the end, tainted from lust.
Paperwork is clutched in the hand,
ready to deliver.
Nerves calm, steady walk, both hands a mere amputation.
A patient bypasses with a spine-tingling shiver.

Sight of sorrow in life and love faced today
when I had to declare to my patient,
"Unfortunately, you've tested positive for AIDS."

Ky Bostick
Hartford, CT

Joseph, the Dreamer Boy

Joseph was young when his dear mother died.
Baby Ben's life spared but not the mother's.
A coat of many colors from his dad
made Joseph the envy of older brothers.

Joseph's dad sent him to check up on them.
They seized him. Into slavery he was sold.
The broken father never learned the truth.
The blood stained coat backed up what he was told.

God works wonders in his mysterious ways
and Joseph was always held in God's hands.
The dreamer boy found favor in the king.
Joseph sold grain to those from dry lands.

Joseph told them to go bring their father
and praised God for giving him so much joy.
The brothers were puzzled by some events.
They realized Joseph was the dreamer boy.

The ten brothers brought their father and Ben
to Goshen where Joseph provided land.
They begged forgiveness for their wrongdoings.
He said to fear not for it was God's plan.

Vera Long
Stillwater, OK

I believe God has a plan for my life, your life, and everyone's life. I believe God intervenes to make dreams a reality. I am ninety-one years old. I give God the credit, as Joseph did, for the miracles in my life. My poems are proof of my faith in God.

The Wave Makers

Rippling through oceans of time
reaching uncharted shores,
offerings, riches beyond
knowledge.

Glistening to the naked eye,
pupils picturing—
For all seasons.

Magnificent humanity
humbleness, timidly, in awe
aware of creator's divinities,
never stopping.

Ripplings, making radiant
presence.

Known and shared,
infinite Helios
cosmic magic—

the wave makers.

Lili Guefen
San Diego, CA

Daughters of Gaia

If ever there was a place in time, it was here and now,
for us to find our place in time.
Barefoot and bold we stood earthing on hallowed ground.
Flowers in our hair and moss stained knees,
lay men and their fathers we ne'er aimed to please.
Women of the wild, we glowed with pride our hearts full
and our eyes wide.
If ever there was a place in time, it was here and now
for us to find our place in time.
We hid under cloak of night, wading in waters made black
by sky and white by moonlight.
Sun dried lavender and rosemary perfumed our skin and babes
clung tight to hip and breast, channeling strength
and love from swollen chest.
We danced as gypsies and cast our spells as we conjured
lightning with swaying hips and parted lips.
Letting rain play upon our burlesque frames we daughters
of Gaia who feel no shame, for we and the tempest are one in
the same.
So if ever there was a time to stake our claim, it is here and now
in this time, by will and strength and with this rhyme.
We daughters of Gaia do mortal men implore, love us,
respect us and fear us once more.

Janine Franklin
Eagan, MN

*I am Janine Franklin, self proclaimed daughter of Gaia. I've been writing poems
and short stories for as long as I can remember. This poem in particular speaks to
me and hopefully many others in more than one way. It's not quite about feminism,
it's not quite about Mother Earth. Though it hints at being about both, to me this
poem is about a longing for a way of life that has always been a lingering ideology
in our world — one where equality isn't just between man and woman or man and
nature, not a coexistence, but evolution into coinherence. It's about respecting the
nature of all things, and relearning to fear the consequences of complacency.*

Linton's Texaco

There once was a special place at the edge of town,
Where "early rising" folks could stop and gather 'round.
They wouldn't be in there long, then have to go.
It was the "loggers'" main fuel stop, Linton's Texaco.

Mrs. Linton would greet everyone with a great big smile.
She'd say come in, get some coffee and let's talk awhile.
The yarns and tales were bigger than one could ever know.
It was the "complete information center," Linton's Texaco.

When the weather was bad outside, real rainy and dark,
The log trucks would be so thick, you could hardly park.
You'd want to go in among that crew real quiet and slow.
You didn't want to miss a word at Linton's Texaco.

Well, them old days are gone, guess it's for the best.
Mrs. Linton is now retired, getting some much needed rest.
The debt of gratitude owed to her, is more than we can show,
For all the early hours spent, at Linton's Texaco.

Gary Thornton
Lufkin, TX

I grew up in the piney woods of deep East Texas in the fifties and sixties. Pulp wood and logging were the major industries of this area at the time. After high school, my dad and I formed our own logging company. We worked together till he retired in '84. Then I took over and worked until I was paralyzed in a log truck accident, in 1988. During my recovery, I started reading a lot and writing simple poetry. I still enjoy doing this and plan to continue in the future!

Spot Inquiry

Actually…
It was excellent
Until
Someone asked me
Just exactly

What

It

Was…
There.

Stephen Kent Odneal
Huntington Beach, CA

My Son, My Son

Strong and sensible with laughing eyes
Lucky me, we have strong ties
Consultant and leader so they say
Working hard every day
A rock as a friend for he has no foes
Warm and friendly he'll give you no woes
Caring and giving are his forte
He makes me happy every single day

Mary Ann Caruso
Laurel, MD

Is This What We Want?

God doesn't love us this I know
Charles Darwin says it's so.
Life evolved from primeval slime
Nullifying God's glorious design.

God doesn't love us this I know
Fredich Nietchie says it's so.
He proclaimed that God is dead
Implying *our* Savior never bled.

God doesn't love us this I know
Everson Court has stated so.
Separation of church and state
Moved our country to a godless fate.

God doesn't love us this I know
Black robed justices made it so.
Roe vs. Wade became our law
Justice made showing man's fall.

God doesn't love us this I know
Supreme Court's decision made it so.
Little ones now face abortion
Why should this become their portion?

God doesn't love us this I know
Family planning makes it so.
Talk of selling babies' parts
Will it break our people's hearts?

Little ones cry out from the womb
Who will save us from the tomb?

Cleo Joppie
Mecosta, MI

Looking out my sliding window, a hummingbird feeder, crab apple tree, and birdbath greet my gaze. A field of wild yellow and pink flowers next appears. Beyond, a line of trees soon to be in brilliant color will soothe my soul.

Eternal Poetry

I do not live as some poets do,
tortured in the shadows,
heart going to the gallows,
writing of dark, storm, the crow.
I don't pour my brokenness on the page
and let my inner struggles rage.
I find true poetry in sunrise;
free verse in the rain.
Limerick in candle wick,
where fires tunes do play.
The sonnets are blue bonnets.
The winds whistle choruses
begging to be heard.
The clouds are cinquain
as they humbly roll by,
not stopping even for the sun
or stars in the sky.
The moon is a story all its own.
The lines written in its good majestic glow.
The mountains are haiku,
as the grass and its dew.
Each written specially,
in God's eternal poetry.

Sarah Danielle Christensen
Carlsbad, NM

Love Is

Love is having laughter and smiles with someone when they are
at their absolute best yet caring enough when they are at their
worst to be sure they know just how much you do love them.
Love is knowing that no matter what unkind words may be said in
moments of anger that apologies for such words are genuine. That
all good times will far outweigh any bad. Love is knowing when to
stay quiet and when to talk til you're blue in the face. It's holding
hands and wiping away tears, it's being sarcastic at times just to
make someone laugh, it's doing all you can for that person because
you want to not because you expect anything in return. Love is
all the small things that turn into big things because of what they
mean. It's knowing that once you're in the other's presence all of
the day's horrible mess just fades away. Love is knowing that for
all your days someone else will always be right there that you can
always depend on. Love is so much more than a word, a feeling or
an action. Yes love is so much more than I could ever explain.

Nicole Lowery
Trenton, TN

*I wrote this poem in dedication to the love I share with my amazing husband
Terry Lowery. He has been my very best friend, my strength when I felt weak,
everything I could ever want in my life partner and so much more. He gives me
the feeling of what love should really be, and I will forever be thankful for that.*

Motivated

Every day I am just doing my thing
Always writing trying to make my way
I am steady trying to make this paper
Don't care what they say
I'm just living my life
I done things I know ain't right I'm steady trying to get that paper
One thing that I am always
Trying to stress is
Never give up when times get hard
Just jot it down
Make that pen leak
Blow these haters off
'Cause you leak your stuff to the public
So if you're doing good
Don't let them waste your time
Since I was like fifteen
I was out here all alone
Had to protect my brother and sister
Also had done it all alone
Now looking back I probably wouldn't
Change a thing
Going through those hard times
Made me who I am today
Made a lot of mistakes
That has taught me a lot of lessons

Thomas Mannstedt
Mounds View, MN

Never Forgotten

Red, white, and patriotic blue,
These colors are what we hold true.
Men and woman of different colors and race,
All come together to protect one place.
A place of freedom,
Home of the brave,
Where people lay down their lives,
And aren't afraid to slay.
We all take for granted minuscule little things,
And we never stop to think about how freedom got its ring.
So let's all take a second,
And put down our cell phones,
To thank our soldiers,
Our veterans at home.
To say just how thankful we are to have this dome,
A place of remembrance and never false hope.
To serve and protect,
So let's make a rope.
One that will unite our country,
Never to be broke.
Thank you our soldiers, veterans, and their friends.
You are all heroes, and we will remember you until the end!

Kayla Davidson
Cape Coral, FL

My Front Porch

On my front porch I sit surrounded by beauty and grace,
And I can't help but think, this is God's place.
Our country of strength, honor and power,
Yet we forget, it could all be gone, in this very hour.

The birds sing their praises and soar with such ease,
As the sunbeams peep through the tall green trees.
Our flag of many stars and stripes waves happily to the neighbors,
The ones who show care and support and bring food as favors.

Yet in the hustle and bustle of this lovely place,
We forget to thank God for his love and his grace.
The neighborly love turns to wars of color and hatred,
And the front porch chatter turns to the topics most debated.

The laughter has grown silent and the tears now flow,
We look for answers, who do we turn to, for many do not know.
Wars have broken out, discrepancies and fighting,
Our soldiers are brave through the bombs that are like lightning.

As I sit on my front porch and think of tomorrow,
Will the days of the future, just bring us more sorrow?
Then I pause to listen, the answer is there,
The birds are still singing and the flag still floats in the air.

The birds, they have no worries and continue in their ways,
For they know the answer, give God all the praise!
So sit on your front porch, breathe in the air,
For this country will be free, as long as God is always there!

Dianna Sharpe
Statesville, NC

I Remember Dad and It Makes Me Sad

I remember Dad how you were
so, so sad and so mad. It was
like yesterday. But so much time,
has kept us so far away. Of a
crime that you gave your life,
to protect your little one's life.
I remember Dad how we saw the
blood shed, as you fell down on
the wooden floor. And we cried
as me and sister watched you
die. 'Cause neither one of us
will get any more of your sweet,
sweet hugs.

Connie Gallimore
Knoxville, TN

My name is Connie Abrams Gallimore, born and raised up in Knoxville, Tennessee—the state of my favorite team, the Vols! I write poems when I'm happy. Writing keeps my mind clear to think. Most of my day to day time is shared with my family, my husband John, daughter Ashley, son Tremaine, and grandbaby Maleigha. They are the important part of wanting to live life. Being published with other poets and writers is an honor to me.

A Memorial Minute

Just is a minute is all they asked
One minute of your time
To close your eyes in thankfulness
Of all they saved for you
The flag that waves above your head
Red and white and blue

Red depicting blood they gave
To keep America free
White depicting pure of heart
Giving of life for thee

Blue depicting future bright
Just for you and me

Remove your hat and show respect
For heroes resting here
They laid their lives upon the line
So you and I could bask
In comfort of our country, great
A minute is all they ask

Janet L. Emery
Sun City, AZ

What Do We Truly Seek

What do we truly seek — hoping to someday find
Could it be the things that elude us most — yet seem
  to constantly occupy our minds

What do we seek — with hope that we will find
A rise to greatness — leaving mediocrity behind
Could it be riches and wealth — kicking poverty aside

For some it may be recognition and fame
And how about the guy who would give anything — if
  people simply would remember his name

What do we seek — hoping to someday find
To rise above the stars — to reach the top of the heap
Maybe even find that love — that is forever to keep

What is it we truly seek — hoping to someday find
For some it may simply be: a "little piece of mind"

Larry Godinho
Sapulpa, OK

Years

How dashing they amass
assembling into ages,
seasons will multiply
with a tree's ring blow.

They hold the fortune
surrendering to no man,
beats as a heart
overcome with eternity.

Yet still we dwell
on its sophistication,
the steadfast dispatching
of imagination blooming.

Ferris Jones
Sparks, NV

I have been published in several magazines and periodicals. Being awarded two grants from the State of Nevada I have published poetry collections entitled Nevada Poets 2009 *and* The Voice of Nevada Poets, *both of which I am credited as editor. I have also published four collections of my own work and run the website www.inquisitionpoetry.com. As a side note I have been the winner of a local poetry contest and have also received recognition for a screenplay entered into* Writer's Digest Magazine's *screen writing contest.*

No Limits

In my days
I never stopped to think
Maybe I don't have a future
Maybe I can't really think
Maybe I'm holding myself back
Maybe there's nothing after this
Maybe I'm nothing

In these years, I tell myself
I am a force in which can't be stopped
I am my past and present
Too creative to be held back
Too loud to be silenced
Everything is behind me
And the nothing in front of me
Is a canvas ready for my painting

A slate in which I can see my mistakes and
Make them successes
A single beat in my song of life
Working with tones and rhythms
For lyrics far beyond comprehension

Gabriella Jurado
Manteca, CA

A Friend of a Friend

The sadness comes upon when there is life lost on our watch
The tears flow freely
Knowing my friend can't see
Feeling that fills with sorrow
Hurt that fills the heart
The mind wanders about
Wondering why I'm still here
Knowing my friend has gone to a quiet place to sleep
As the mind "mine" has not slept
Seeing the results of the accident
As time comes and goes, I will remember the hurt
And one day it will depart
I will be stronger for all to see

Dorothy Ann McFarlane
Maynard, MA

Little Things

As relationships grow older, we become complacent.

We allow our minds to be consumed with unimportant day to day things.

Result! We forget the little things that are so important to our relationships.

Like a hug, for no reason, a note tucked in to a pocket, a squeeze of the hand as you pass by, saying I love you, I'm sorry, or that was my fault, a smile across a crowded room. Little things, but oh, so important.

It is sad we become so consumed with the unimportant things in our life, that we let our loved ones slip to the back of our minds.

Our excuses: we're so busy. But the one you love is more important and before it's too late, take a few minutes from your day to make sure they know you care, before it's too late.

It is the most important time of your life.

So take the time, as time is the most important and precious gift you can give for that person may not be here tomorrow and you will forever regret, that you did not take time for the little things.

Cecelia Smith-Cameron
Wainwright, AB

I love to write and I get ideas from listening to others and from my own experiences. I know from experience: don't delay, it just may be too late.

Remembering the Beacon Ferry

Beacon New York flared orange and
Collapsed, bronzing the future site
Of Riverfront Memorial Park
Donated by Pete and Toshi Seeger
As the sun crept into the Sha-Wan Gunk Mountains.

I came up here from Ossining
After three of two to five
With a kite for Brew Mulqueen's wife.

There across the Hudson a ferry
Captain rammed and sunk Newburgh.
Its welfare citizenry spewed out
To wash ashore at Monachie, New Jersey.

Shoulders hunched against the breeze
Along the Taconic State, beyond Walkiln.
Into the darkness of the Berkshires.
Marriage.   Purgatory.

Judd Plumbly
Williamsburg, WV

Hummingbirds

Have you ever wondered where hummingbirds go
  When the rain and the wind so furiously blow?
Do they hide in the crook of the old oak tree?
  Do they lean on the safe side of a chimney?
Do they have a nest somewhere, snug and warm,
  Where they can wait out the furious storm?

Are they borne on the gusts of the wind so strong
  To faraway places that they've never known?
Are they crushed by the strength of the falling rain,
  And cannot rise on their wings again?
Have you ever wondered where hummingbirds go
  When the rain and the wind so furiously blow?

There is a story in God's wonderful word
  How He cares for the sparrow, and each little bird
So they find resting places to weather the storm,
  And afterward fly where it's sunny and warm,
Basking in sunlight through the day's lazy hours…
  Joyfully feeding in fields of wildflowers.

So you see, there's a plan… God cares for His own…
  All the animals and birds that we've ever known.
All the world He created, all the heavens above
  Are guided and guarded by His wonderful love.
So don't be afraid when you weather the storm…
  God will carry you through… where it's sunny and warm.

Yvonne E. Cole
Villa Rica, GA

Free Me

…you hear me? you hear me… you can do more… I know you can…
it's going on in the back of my head
"again you should fiend" is what he said
you are a God amongst the red
ants from the dirt those demons you shed
be the evil for the greater good take one step
to the thousand mile journey, search it on Craig's
list no you won't get what he picks
out is his brain it drains listen close hear the dead
you can treat how you want to
conceive it how you want to
believe it if you want to eat if you want to
seek if you want to
he won't leave it but he wants to
take it, mold it, shape it, shake it, grab his gift, manipulation
use it for the sick and, patient, if he could not, change it, break it!
…but it would put his ego in starvation
a man-made craving, he gets what he wants
the inner battle beats the brain into greatness
…but it would put his ego in starvation
a man-made craving, he gets what he wants!
the inner battle beats the brain into greatness!
free me, free me

Elijah Baranyk-Smith
Milwaukee, WI

I'm a simple man fighting his inner demons that say, "Free me."

Life Among the Giants

From those who live among the giants
One might expect complete compliance
And not instead yawning defiance
Accompanying entitled reliance
Thus is the nature of feline dance
Susceptible giants fall entranced
Wishing to please and appease each glance
Delighted by a destructive prance
Actions of cats among the giants
Must not be seen as male-fi-cence
Causing captors to withdraw their grants
And toss them out among shrubs and plants
To fend with ferals, grubs and ants
And end upon coyote's lance
For from the time of the pharaoh hence
Cats have been man's best defense
Against insidious arrogance
Having scaled the top of Nature's fence
And in spite of disobedience —
Thinking the mother takes no offence
At behavior clearly malevolent —
Man lives to wreak more hinder-ance
Why no earthly retali-ance?
Maybe 'cause cats crave his presence
Purrfect two paws up benevolence
Through unconditional acceptance

Patricia Austin
Cape Cod, MA

Love Struck, Once

Like the hands of time
Figures on a clock,
Love dances around a face that never tires,
Of seeing two hands
Come together for a brief moment,
Only to drift apart.

Jodi-Kay Edwards
De Pere, WI

Tall Truth

orange crushed moon tequila
heads back, burnt throats, sour faces
getting drunk (you not me)
knowing you're doing it to tell me
what you'll think I'll forget in the morning
closing in on your secrets
and the space between our legs
fragmented sentences
clacking tongues
inside our dehydrated mouths
you stared too long
and I melted into your eyes
forgive me

Jennifer Bleich
North Liberty, IA

Weeping Willow

Weeping willow dry your tears
Don't be afraid
Don't hide away

You don't understand why she left
You didn't get to say goodbye
Oh poor weeping willow

You will see it will be alright
Just not today
But maybe someday
The sun will rise again

Oh sweet weeping willow
Remember her smiling face
Cling to the memories
The memories will last forever

Whitney Engle
Calvert City, KY

Whispers of Love

When it's all said and done
and your time has come

It's whispers of love in the moonlight
whispers of love into the daylight

Whispers of love it's all from above
it's whispers of love to the twilight

We hear your whispers Momma
we feel your whispers Momma

You tell us it's your time
it's whispers of love in the moonlight

Can't believe your time is here Momma
it's whispers of love in the daylight

You tell us of the other side
it's whispers of love in the twilight

We will forever love you Momma
it's whispers of love in the daylight

Deb Jackson
Fargo, ND

As Cool As the Wind

In the midst of changes
my love I will send
Though around you it seems
as cool as the wind
When the night is calling
and snow has fallen deep
Ice maids skirt the window
the gardens gone to sleep
But only for a season
renewal is in the plan
Our earth will be a garden
for the woman and the man
Though Eden's at your doorstep
is coming just 'round the bend
the seasons all are turning
as cool as the wind
It's time for Heaven's season
the children clap and sing
Their angel wings are beating
are anxious for a change
So while the world grows weary
and foes outweigh the friend
a refreshing breeze is blowing
as cool as the wind

A refreshing breeze is blowing

as cool as the wind

Laurie Plymale
Carlisle, PA

In November of 2001, just weeks after the sad events of 9/11, my nana contacted me in a dream. She had passed away seven years earlier. She came to me with a poem and handed it to me. When I awoke, I wrote it down. I believe our loved ones watch over us and dreams are a perfect meeting place. This poem is a gift and I'll treasure it always. May we all be guided by the loving spirits of our loved ones. In doing so, may we have that special world we all dream of.

Forevermore

Once again
The unknown is all there is

Two years later
That's all

That's all you get
That's all that's left
That's all we have time for

Time
It ticks by
Like the bomb that it is

One more step

Out the door
That's all we have time for

No more

Hannah N. Roberts
Ringgold, GA

I Walk the Streets

There was a time I walked the streets alone,
The world living and moving all around me.
People coming and going, buying and selling,
And I wandered aimlessly here and there, to and fro.
I tried to blend so I would not feel alone.
Tried blending in uncomfortable awkward situations,
To rid the feeling of emptiness and loneliness.

Still searching, I joined a crowd into a building.
My heart beat as it never had beat before.
I felt joy and peace and a love unspeakable.
It was unlike anything I had known,
As if hearing words for the first time,
As if seeing life take color,
As if being a part of a family.

Feeling of loneliness seemed to vanquish.
Words that were spoken filled my emptiness.
This place was like no other,
There was no alone or fear,
I heard the calling that my heart longed for,
I found Jesus my savior!

I walk the streets these days,
But I never walk alone!

Theresa L. Quarshie
Fort Smith, AR

Sifting Sand in Ole Mesquite

The streets are wide and no one's in sight
Some of the folks work through the night
It's a three-shift day in this resort town
People come to gamble from miles around
The Mormons chose these plateaus steep
To plant their crops and tend their sheep
The Virgin River was a challenge to all
Cresting waters through their new town hall
Might and God and will found way
And the town got stronger day by day
Lights came on and telephones were heard
We're getting stronger was the latest word
A tourist shop brought truckers in
To gas up and see if they could win
Word got out about this quiet place
That's what started the big land race
"We don't mind progress but do it right
Plan it well so we won't have to fight
It's a challenge to keep a little town small
When someone's talking about building a mall
Crossing the street is not the same
With someone rushing to a poker game
Desert hills sport a new golf course
On the spot where I used to feed my horse
Gambling is here with the good and the bad
So toss the dice and put it on my tab"

Charlotte C. McLaughlin
Lakewood, CO

Hoonda

Hoonda, our Cathoula hound, her
protecting bark, a welcome sound,
is with the angel dogs above, who
continue to bless our lives with
their angel dog love.

I miss her bark and her crazy eyes,
and her posture with the way a hound
dog lies. She has her own needs,
and every day, she let us know in
her own special way.

Now she rests in the backyard in her
own open space, I'm putting a
bench nearby for a meditation
place. Dogs teach us lessons, I'm
sure it is true, by the way that
they live and the things that they do.

Some dogs are man's best, truest
and most loyal friend, their sentinel
spirit continuing to guard us to
our own life's end.

Jo Ann M. Hayden
Bend, OR

Thank You

Brought tears to my eyes to see you open your eyes,
You did.
Brought home unity, love, caring, the light of life,
You did.
Chased away days of worry with your first birthday,
You did.
I wiped pride filled tears away graduation day,
I did.
Brought smiles to marry you at the end of the aisle,
It did.
Brought new smiles home with my beautiful grandchild
You did.
Like a sudden clap of thunder you were "Mama,"
You kid.
No father could be prouder of all that you did,
Thank you kid.

Michael Gordon Moore
Santa Clarita, CA

Human Shield

You were my human shield,
protecting my soul
from the bombardments of life.

You were my human shield
saving me from the onslaught
of relentless shelling.

I moved you about
to protect me
in my weakest spots.

But, like any captive,
I, your captor,
became involved
and could no longer
loosen my attachment.

The human shield I had used
to protect me,
began to confuse me
and I became unsure
who was falling in
the shadow of whom.

I needed to reclaim my shadow,
so I opened up myself to the shelling
and discovered I could survive
while you, a weary captive,
returned home.

Anne Croly
Bronx, NY

9/11

Never forget 9/11
It will always remind us that horrible day
The pain of loss will remain forever
And grief, that entire nation has paid.
…I stepped with other people on the ground,
I see many different faces.
And only one expression around—
Honor and sadness, like in no other places.
Memorial pools placed on the ground,
And thousand names have been printed on the wall.
Those people—I think about—
Young, healthy—they're gone, all of them…
Time is flying and children are growing,
Some visit the ground and read parents' names.
We never forgive, we always will know—
Our heroes—remember them all!

Marina Malinskaya
Brooklyn, NY

Undone

Unjaded by my contact with the world,
Fresh, and cherishing my newness
(As I could not do when I was born,)
Awed by colors that I see and
Shapes that sing diversity.

No, I am not timeworn.

I hear the music of the universe,
And bathe in its symphonic beat,
There is so much that is undone,
Yet knowing I can only taste so much
Sensations limited to my touch

Remind me that I am only one.

But, oh, the generosity that made
The world so alive for more than me,
Exciting others even more than I
To know the beauty of the sky,
The newness of it all, as seen and felt
Through babies yet unborn, who grow
To know the joy in being one,

Who see connections in things undone.

George V. Neagu
Michigan City, IN

Desert Rose

Desert Rose how is it that you bloom so
beautifully in a barren land?

How is it that your fragrance is so sweet
where your roots grow and stand?

You are a true life expression
of the *great majestic creator's hand.*

Desert Rose which blooms
in a barren land.

Mollie Frost
Sparks, NV

What I Can Be for You

Over a year I've waited for you,
To show what makes a real woman.
Unselfish, caring, self-secured, independent, respectful,
  trustworthy, dorky when I'm with you.

I'm that woman, let me show you what I've been wanting to
  share with you.
I won't hurt you and that's the truth.

Kelli Magaña Magaña
Fillmore, CA

The Drone Drones On

Little drone
Flying high in the sky
What do you see
As you fly by?
Do you see me
Get undressed
If you do
This causes me distress!
Do you see me
All a flutter
As I smear my toast
With peanut butter
Or do you see
Our secret service
Acting like they're
Really nervous?
Little drone
Up high in the sky
What are you looking
For as you fly by?
Are you looking
For strategy in
Our government's hand
Well don't waste your time
There is no plan!
So little drone
Drone on with your laser
And get out of our sight
It would give us pleasure!

Wilmetta Feezor
Indianola, IL

I am an eighty-two-year-old grandmother. I have three children: a daughter Nancy (Wes) Grimer, a son Dan (Jenny) Freezor and another daughter Dr. Lori (Ben) Ribble. I have two grandsons and three granddaughters. I also have five step-grandchildren: two boys and three ladies. I am also writing a book.

Election Day

My name is Mother Goose with a problem to see through
Just be kind of neutral and give my point of view
The animals were all restless and all began to stew
Trying to find a leader to head that barnyard crew
Everyone had their opinion of what they all should do
Someone had to lead them and be fair about it too
The horse neighed his opinion and he threw in a shoe
The pigeon gave his answer, he said, let's just bill and coo
The rooster he was ready when he got up and flew
Then put in a short straw for the hen that he would woo
The cow got into the act having her cud to chew
She voted for the rooster when she gave one big moo
The goat and the capon they didn't have a clue
Leaving it to the others with what they all knew
The place was going crazy as the tension really grew
The whole bunch was fighting, the place was like a zoo
It lasted through the night until the morning dew
They still had no one picked but all had named a few
The sow had not been asked as she lay there in the goo
She pulled out a long straw and voted for the gnu
Where did he come from, they all said with a boo
Because he just arrived here and he is way too new
Then they got real serious and tightened the old screw
Giving a straw to each animal wondering what they drew
The votes were all counted and many of them were blue
The animal with the most votes was the fluffy little ewe

Marvin Hitzemann
Waterloo, IL

Before Love Could Bloom

Water rushes down the sidewalk
Tears flow down her face and are licked up by the rain.
Her sobs are drowned out by the rumbling of thunder,
Sorrow engulfs her body leaving her prisoner.
She collapses against a nearby dumpster,
The tin cries out in protest.
Why her? What did she do to deserve such pain?
She pounds her fist on the dumpster
Her screams echo up into the empty world
No one listens. No one cares.
She feels a sudden, sharp pain in her palm
A single, withered rose dangles from her skin.
Frustrated, she rips the flower from her hand
Crimson blood trickles down her arm
Each drop causing ripples in the water below.
She holds the rose tightly and gazes down at it
Once so loved and cherished, now tossed away like trash.
No one remembers the beauty it once held
Or the joy it once gave,
No one cares.
She crushes the beloved flower just as he did her heart.
She tosses it onto the sidewalk and watches it drown.
It is left lying there, a victim to the cruel world
Lifeless, torn apart and alone
Just like her.

Karli Robertson
Sunderland, ON

How Does Teaching Make You Feel

Teaching makes me feel that I am learning
About others: their need, their
    aspirations, their
    uniqueness as individuals.
About myself: the realization that
    I continue to grow.
Teaching makes me feel that I am sharing
    the knowledge which has come to me
    from the past.
Teaching makes me feel that I am guiding
    the inexperienced toward new horizons.
Teaching makes me feel that some small
    part of me is woven into the
    history of mankind.

Jeanette Olmstead
Grants Pass, OR

When I was in my forties, I went to college to become a teacher. In my education class, the teacher asked this question: "How does teaching make you feel?" I graduated when I was fifty.

My Daughter, My Life

Her laugh rings through me
like a thousand bells.
The soft sweet way
her little head smells.

Her smile so bright,
her giggle so sweet.
Her precious tiny fingers,
her chubby little feet.

What filled my days before,
I do not know.
I've so much love within me,
from inside my heart I glow.

A beautiful new world
has just begun.
For in it, is my beautiful daughter
so precious and pure.

Kathy Lorentz
McCook, NE

Know One

The leaves swirl
around your head
as confusion sets in.
Love, hate—it all
blends into one. No
one hears the cries
for help, the tears of pain are never
wiped away. The never-ending
years of mental abuse go
unanswered. You are
the brunt of the jokes. The laughter is
all on you. Whatever
is wrong is all on you. Anyone
can put you
down; no one lifts you
up. You are the ugly, fat,
dumb one. You can no longer look
in the mirror without
seeing what is truly there.
You try and try but you can
never satisfy. More and more
is taken until only
a shell remains. You are
the true living
dead. The leaves
swirl around your head.

Celia Nieves
Bradenton, FL

Savior from Insanity

The world is spinning 'round and 'round
My vision is blurry, I'm feeling down
There's a storm in my head, and holes in my heart
And right now everything's falling apart

The wind is blowing, pushing me around
The world is crumbling, cracks in the ground
Everything is falling from around my feet
I spread my arms wide, close my eyes, admit defeat

As I start falling, and accept the end
A hand grabs my arm and pulls me back in
I look up at the man who saved my life
The darkness cleared and there was light

The world stopped spinning and fell back into place
The insanity stopped, this ended the chase
And to the man, the debt I can't repay
I've stayed with him to this very day

Jacquelyn R. Torres
Stoughton, MA

True Colors

Color is everywhere
Living and dead
Spurting from
People's fingertips, mouths,
Thoughts
Remnants and fragments
Are still alive with
Color
People's minds, souls…
Filled with color
Vibrant, neon, pastels,
Or monochrome…
Colors disguise and reveal
When mixed, mingled,
With another
Results are clear or muddled
Dead colors are simply waiting
A snatch fluttering in the breeze
A sparkle trampled in the streets
Waiting for a different interest
Waiting for rebirth
Quietly dreaming
To be a new color

Charlotte George
Paola, KS

What People See

What do they see, the outsiders who
Watch as my dad walks down the street?
He sways and teeters, but doesn't fall.
He is looking around, but doesn't quite see it all.
"He looks drunk," I tell my mom.
She completely agrees.
That's probably how he looks to everyone else,
To those who cannot see —
Cannot see the illness that has taken his body,
The one that has also taken his mind.
I know he is not drunk, and I do what I can to help him.
I doubt a police officer who saw him walking would be so kind.
The officer doesn't see. No one sees.
My dad is not drunk.
He has Huntington's disease.

Alyssa Gass
Manteca, CA

In Memory of Michael James Robertson

(September 17, 1975–November 30, 2010)

It is your birthday today,
We miss you more than we did yesterday
Even though you are where God wants you to be
It was way too soon to let you leave this earth or your family

Your mom and dad are still so sad
Jaelyn and your sisters are just as bad
You were wiser than your years by date
To say, "If my child colors on the wall, I'll color with her,"
    instead of berate

Your smile lit up everyone's life
Always with a joke and never spite
You could tear things apart and put them back together again
That was a true love of an auto mechanic's heart

Life eventually has to move on, but tears still flow
When they play those special songs
"Here Comes the Son" and "Grandpa Tell Me 'Bout the Good
    Old Days"
Oh so pain free and playing your guitar

Let me make this "Crystal" clear
We are all just waiting to join you there…
No "Ring of Fire" will greet you here
You will be the king fisherman with all your gear

You light up the night,
By being the brightest star
We will all see you again someday
So open your arms and lie in wait

Loraine Yousse
Cedar Rapids, IA

Because of You

Been through most of my life but somehow I got lost
The price that I paid far too great was the cost
Always lonely and sad trying hard just to cope
With your care and concern found a line with a rope
I keep holding on tight though my way's long and weary
Looking forward to days when my road's not so dreary
My fear though is time, as it passes me by
Hard to stop for that reason just wondering why
"Need to pull yourself up!" my inner self *screams…!*
Not so easy to do when you've lost all your dreams
Yet, the struggles, steps taken, though baby ones too
Strength received, hope felt comfort all *because of you*
I know, it's not easy so most people do say
Changes made can come only as I struggle along my way
Finding me, hard to do but still holding on tight
Yet, with you as a guide hopeful changes in sight
See, an angel's been sent; her gentle sound is so clear
Forever her presence, forever so near
My life to make sense will stem from her power
My days overwhelming, I tread hour to hour
So, thank you most dear one who's linked to me so
I'll hold on to your rope and will never let go
Because of you and the "who" that you are
I find inner peace will aim high for a star
Because of you too, my world a better place
Envisioning my angel, I see Cathy's face

Janet Suchorski
Weymouth, MA

I know it is impossible to choose family members, yet, if I could only one comes to mind. Always present as really no other, she is the strong link that keeps me whole. I smile, cry, but my hope keeps me balanced and it is because of her. She knows too well the place where I came from — how, when and why. I may wander away but I feel a constant force keeping me focused. "Because of You" for this reason is dedicated to Cathy, my "chosen" family member.

Raindrops

You're joyful to my ears
I am so glad you're here
you make things green
and you make pretty
things and you make
the leaves dance with joy
and you make tomatoes big
and round and fruit and
vegetables by the pound
and when I hear you on
the roof it's a beautiful
sound and when I hear
that little drip-drip on
the windowpane it
makes me want to dance
to your sweet sound

Jack Johnson
Charlotte, MI

When Is It Going to End?

When is it coming
to an end?

When will this
seemly unquenchable thirst
for violence and discord
end?

What will make it stop?
Stricker gun control laws
and fingerprinting.

What will we do?
As people listen to a
bagpipe being played. The tune
of "Amazing Grace" filled the
air.

Jonita Jett
Knoxville, TN

Sorrow for Tomorrow

I keep waiting for someday
Still wading in hopes and dreams
When is that day coming my way
'Cause that day never comes it seems

I have to get through these hard times
I'm facing these times on my own
So cry with me until the sun shines
And don't let me die here alone

Now I'm dancing real close to the edge
To stay balanced I just don't down
And I can't get this sad song out of my head
'Cause my sorrow is crying too loud

And I'm only feeling lonely
When on the brink of despair
I really need someone to hold me
Someone to shield me from the glare

Billy Hitz
Margate, FL

She Loves Baskets

We have a kitty that loves to sleep in baskets, with few around the house that she has discovered, would be commandeered by her. That was the place to be where she likes to sleep and watch TV. But when it came to eat, she'd dash to the kitchen for a treat as she'd wait patiently at her plate.

Then her ears would perk up to the sound of the snapping lid, out of can of her favorite dish, three fish delight. Oh, what a sight! Dinner was served. She would look up at me with a grin from ear to ear and a nod of the head, as to say thank you dear.

With a wink of her eye, back to her basket she went, and sat up as straight as can be: looking for affection and to be as pleasing as one kitty could be.

In her pastime she'd be on the windowsill attempting to catch the birds, butterflies and bees as they went swooping and zooming and buzzing at her head.

It was a very a-mew-zing sight as she was inside, looking out. This little kitty would try to swat through the windowpane, as she try to catch them passing by.

This was quite the sport and tiring activity as any kitty can take. She'd look around and scan the room to find her favorite wicker basket to sleep. Where she felt comfort, for this was the place to be, away from dog and flea.

Paula C. Drown
Monroeville, OH

My poem is about my kitty cat Fuzzy Moto, a beautiful and amazing feline friend who was born with one eye, her other coral blue. Fuzzy's coat is caramel and white. She keeps it very clean. When Fuzzy was a baby kitten she was abandoned by her mother on a snowy cold field on a February day in 2011. We, my husband Lyn and I, rescued her, brought her in our home and attended to her needs. To this day she has been an affectionate and humorous kitty with gratitude. At this very moment she is in her basket watching TV.

To Reunite

A sand dollar has washed away and reached the shore.
A journey reached through the rhythm of glistening waves and
gliding over sand so pure.
Filled with memories of the blue horizon and treasures of the heart.
A light house has always guided the way.
Some bodies of water were turbulent.
Some as warm as the sun.
There were storms and serenity,
Lightning and the tide.
The water is shared and reunites.
The rest of the journey is through ever changing footprints upon
rainbow reflected sands.
The pearls of the ocean must remain where they are.
Reaching the shore there are no dark waters.
The gardens are eternal and beautiful.
Whirlwinds of spirits on boundless flights.
A shell remains in this world.
Each and every part of the journey will be forever unbroken.
A sand dollar has washed away and reached the shore...

Sherry Grimm
Komono, IN

A Grandmother's Love

She was with you from the start of your life.
You were with her at the end of her strife.

She is now watching you from above
Sending down all of her grandmotherly love.

She will be at each and every game
Cheering for you with the call of your name.

Her voice so proud that I hope you can hear it.
She's with us now if only in spirit.

You filled her with pride each and every day
For it was in this life that she wanted to stay.

Her pain was too great and she had to surrender
Now leaving us all with a love so tender.

She loved you all for who you are
So honor her love and become her star.

Lori Schmitt
Fort Wayne, IN

I Am Loved

I want to climb to the top of the mountain
I want to hear the echo of my voice ring on forever
I want to stretch up and whisper to each star
And I want to talk to the moon face to face
I want to tell the sun how warm I feel inside
I want to touch every tree and let it sway to the rhythm in my soul
I want to hear the birds singing of my love
I want to turn over every rock and tell everything underneath
And I want to tell the world that, I am loved

Judith Marsh
Uniondale, PA

My husband was away at work for an extended period. I was alone and decided to climb the mountain behind our house, which I did often. All of these thoughts and ideas kept coming to me through everything I gazed upon. I was so inspired, I came down and wrote this poem.

What's Seen and Unseen

You ask what I see when I close my eyes
Why, there! Yesterday's so stunning, golden sunrise
You see, while looking over memory,
I see the past is here with me
And only the future lies still, unseen

Bridget Ingraham
Phoenix, AZ

Scars

I knew a boy who liked to draw
He drew sketches that nobody saw
His hands would clench to almost white
Alone in his room where his imagination would ignite
He kept his drawings to himself
And let his secret grow dusty on a faraway shelf
His drawings were different, no pad nor quill
But these drawings were slowly beginning to kill
Instead of dripping ink that would glisten
The point of his pen was splashed with crimson
We stood by the river gazing at Mars
He rolled up his sleeves and revealed his scars
And that was when he made his secret ours

Lizzi M. Cronin
Weston, MA

Hush

Light—
>   moves over
>>   the quiet earth
>>>   on a breath, shining
>>>>   gulps-of-air part cloud…

Joh Cambilargiu
Tooele, UT

For me, these are thoughts rolling along on an easy breath, reflecting nature, taking pause…

God Talked to Me

It was something so fantastic
That it will never be forgotten
God actually came to talk to me
And opened my eyes so I could see

What I saw was so very wonderful
God gave to me an entire new life
One needn't approve how others live
Love and compassion is what you give

Those were words the Almighty did send
It made me know, God is my best friend!

Mary Jean Tull
Pekin, IL

December 2000

Silence, stillness
No sound breaks through the emptiness.
No moon, no stars; only dark clouds over dark woods,
Shades of black and grey,
Fields of blue grass under dark skies,
Asphalt streets glistening wet,
Lifeless, tall buildings.
Nothing moves.

This is the way the promise ends?
Nukes, bugs, chemicals?
What made the earth go dead?

Two millennia of expectations
Dashed
The massive Gothic cathedrals
Crumbling into dust.

Periodic revivals promised Christ would come.
Maranatha,
Only His arrival would make it all worthwhile:
All the wars, suffering, morality, righteous faith.
But now it's all finished,
And Jesus never came.

Thomas Chevraux
Canton, OH

Old Glory

Old Glory waving in the breeze
    Way up high above the trees
Stars and stripes—red, white and blue
    Our God, we give our thanks to You

For peace and freedom in our land—
    Blessing from Your mighty hand
For brave young men who fight and die
    To keep Old Glory flying high

Oh God, please bless the USA
    With men of faith who live Your way,
To lead this land of the free and brave
    And all our treasured freedoms save

Christine O'Rear
Rossville, GA

I was sitting on the porch July 4, 2014, watching the flag waving in the breeze and thinking how blessed I am to be a citizen of the greatest nation in the world, the United States of America! I am eighty-one years old and was raised to respect the flag and what it stands for. I always get goose bumps when I see it waving so proudly.

I Believe in Miracles

I believe in miracles, so I listen when God calls,
For he has performed so many for me,
I could never count them all.
I know about the miracles of Christ
And how he healed the lame,
And before he could rest awhile,
He did the blind the same.
I have to believe in miracles,
For I could never never explain,
How the things I've asked of him,
Are given over and over again.
Yes, I believe in miracles, for I've learned the life of Christ.
How he came to love us, by giving holy sacrifice.
If you believe in miracles, and have visions of things to come,
You must first trust in him and have love for everyone.
Yes, I believe in miracles and that healing is divine,
And the power of the Holy Spirit is not at all confined.
I truly believe there are miracles,
Christ's resurrection tells me so,
I'll keep on believing that I'll be receiving and
Let my God know.

Virginia L. Boone
Virginia Beach, VA

This is one of my favorite poems. I am not writing as I used to. I write mainly for my church, New Genesis Baptist Church. Our pastor is Melvin Cotton Jr., MA MDiv.

I Am Child

I am child
    Imagination is my age
        Needs are few
            Wants are many

I have a fear
    I know a monster
        It lives within me
            I feel It moving through and about me

It knows the unknown darkness
    There is no monster Momma says
        But I know It — It knows me
        It wants me

Before sleep vanquishes my fears or when sleep evades
    It is there
        It comes to me
            It stays — so close

It frightens me — then I'm scared!

I am child
    Ageless
        Imagination is my age

Robert C. Lory
Burlington, WI

This poem is for you, Emily Pirkle — queen of the universe. Truly you are the most beautiful and brightest of all the stars in the heavens and the one upon whom I shall make my wishes forever! You have my eternal gratitude for bringing your light to the darkness. Remember me.

Red

My arms bear scars and secrets,
of untold truths and you.
The unbroken sky
tastes like sorrows,
so many whispers in the trees.
I can count them
my footsteps,
trace them to the moon.
Spin around, arms out wide
don't let them know
what's inside.
Maybe it's just what I can't forget,
maybe it's just me.
Soft glowing streetlights,
gentle flowing tears.
Hush now child, hide the tiny rivers.
My heart hides burdens I can't share,
of little things, corrosive lies.
I can stop them
my feelings,
halt them for the end;
tear into my life
to live again.
Until the storm raging around me is finally larger
than this terrible never ending one inside.

Janina Kylie Ritzen
Surrey, BC

Diamonds in the Rough

These are my diamonds and my pearls
Three handsome guys and three gorgeous girls.

I have no rings on my fingers
Because I raised six wonderful stinkers.

They were given to me as a gift from God.
No other gift could be more precious than this lot.

I enjoyed and treasured these valuable stones
As I nurtured and helped with the development of their bones.

They have a beauty, all of their own,
What shining sparkle they have shown.

They most definitely increased in value, as the years have passed.
For surely no other stone could ever be surpassed.

Their brilliant nature and loving ways,
Will outshine the brightest diamond of our days!

Anna Kuzmich
Lewisville, TX

At my granddaughter's wedding shower in 2008, the ladies around the table were proudly displaying their diamonds on their fingers. All I had was a solid gold wedding band. Suddenly I had a flash back about a poem I had written years ago, titled "Diamonds in the Rough," in 2004. There they were bragging about the diamonds on their fingers. How uncanny is that? I am now eighty-six years old and still have no diamonds on my fingers — only in my heart.

He's Coming Back

No man knows the day or hour
When Christ the Lord will come in power,
And when He does, all heads will bow,
And knees will bend; that is His vow

As promised with a trumpet blast,
Old Satan's power will end at last,
Jesus brings his kingdom here,
A new heaven and earth will then appear

He's coming back, the Bible tells the story
He's coming back in the twinkling of an eye,
He's coming back in power and in glory
He's coming back with angels by his side!

Brian W. Jerden
Peculiar, MO

Metals of Honor

She once saw a beautiful face,
    lines now show within that place.
Each line has a story to tell
    and each line she knows the story so well.
Sad and happy come to mind
    and each one she has gone over many times.
Some lines are from total despair
    before that time she doesn't remember them being there.
But others are from happier times
    ascending upward with smiles sublime.
And as she looks into her weathered mirror
    her heart begins to swell.
Oh yes, she has earned those lines so well.
And like metals of honor,
    lines embedded into her face,
she wears her metals of honor with style and grace.

Cecilia Hattendorf
Hesperia, CA

Have You Noticed?

Have you taken the time
to sit still and listen?
Have you noticed
how the world behaves?
Have you felt the sway
of insects and beasts,
smelled the power
of moon and stars,
heard the echo
of standing trees,
seen the calm
of windy nights?
Have you known
the tug of nature,
the pull of loved ones dear?
Have you felt the
meditative seductiveness
of peace by a calm river in the night?
Have you noticed
the little moments
that we all take for granted,
but make life perfect?
Have you noticed the little things,
slight imperfections that make anyone
perfect the way they are?

Tanner Lloyd
Salt Lake City, UT

My Petunia

It is those golden eyes with
silk black and with orange iridescent
patched fur, finally paired with an
illuminated white tipped tail that
I adore. Her spontaneous glitches
of unrelenting curiosity only shadow
her deep longing for a better sense of
adventure. In a sense you perceive
an almost feeling of being watched
by some shadow figure, which from
my perspective is true. She has an
absolute passion for creative havoc
and chaotic events, but she also
has her calm and precious times
as well. Her ingenious acts of solving
how to type and create a password
are both funny plus peculiar. To say
that my kitten is cute is an
understatement, rather it is that she
is the most uniquely personified cat
that I have ever met. I just love
her, my Petunia.

Amanda M. Nickey
Alta Loma, CA

To Be Published

The wind blows across the hills
The little house stands
Awaiting its downfall
As of yet it stands tall

It awaits its fate
For one day it may topple
Down, down the hill
Those stilts only last so long

The girl inside
She sits at her desk
Awaiting her downfall
As she covers the page

Writing her letters
She waits for the end
Though she knows not when it comes
The ruse can only last so long

Molly O'Scannell
Anchorage, AK

God Said, "Let It Go"

There are times of great temptation.
There are times of condemnation.
These are times of weakness;
God says strive for the power of meekness.

Let it go and feel the freedom.
Let it go and feel the calm.
All your strifes and all your struggles
Aimed toward others, will be gone.

No need to worry,
No need to fear
For I am always,
Always near!

I said, "I cannot let it go.
I try, and I try, and I try… but
My perceptions of others robs me of my peace…
And time goes by."

He said, "Let it go,
Your anger will disappear
Lean on me,
No others instead."

Let it go?
Because?
"Because!"

"I said."

Deanna L. Payne
Holland, MI

A Mother's Way

Let me hold your hand in mine
While I still can.
For before I blink my eyes,
You'll be a man.
Let me wipe your tear shed eyes
While I stand above.
For before I turn my head
You will be the person you were meant to be.
There is no other way
That I can care for you,
Than this loving way
All mothers will surely do.
Let me hold you in my arms
While you're still mine.
The years will fly and,
You'll be grown and it will be
A memory of what was once,
When you were mine.

Nanci Mascia
Mayfield Heights, OH

I Write This Poem

Thoughts keep dancing through my head,
Things I've thought, things I've said;
Things I've heard, things I've read,
A poem screams out to me.

Can silence be found among the chatter,
Among the clings, clangs and clatter;
Boings, bangs and bug's splatter,
A poem screams out to me.

Will music tame the savage beast,
A lion, tiger, wildebeest;
Playing joyfully… a love feast,
A poem screams out to me.

Joy-filled songs and silly laughter,
Living life with each new chapter;
Gliding, sailing, feeling rapture,
A poem screams out to me.

Thoughts keep dancing through my head,
Things I've thought, things I've said;
Things I've heard, things I've read,
A poem screams out to me.

Marlene Daley
Roseburg, OR

Untitled

You were an inspiration that only
stopped itself
You were always there for a
shoulder to cry on
You truly were such a great
friend and mother
While you are gone we know that
you are looking on us from above
You have brought an infectious
smile to the ones that have all loved you
We will never forget how much you
meant
May you rest in peace through
these ashes that are set

Stephen M. Hawkins
Florence, SC

I am twenty-five years old, the second son of Jeff and Peggy Hawkins. I have two brothers, Chris and Kevin. We live in Florence, SC. I have cystic fibrosis, a life-threatening illness. To help me deal with all that CF entails, I write poetry as a form of therapy. When in the hospital, I will write poems for the staff. This poem was written as a tribute to Grandma Hawkins. I wrote this poem the morning of her memorial service, the words coming quickly to my mind. This poem was read by me at my grandmother's memorial.

Licence to Voyage West: Oh Canada

On a travelling bus across the vast maple leaf land,
Je me souviens,
The blue Lys flowers and a distinct cultural identity.
Yours to discover,
The Queen's landmark crowns this multicultural mecca of Masala;
Certainly, I feel foreign this land of my birthplace.
Friendly,
Aboriginals: I am among the natives of this land.
Land of the living skies,
Farms and hay bales. The flat lands extend forward endlessly.
Wild Rose Country,
South skies light up the land of the cowboys at night,
Further North a massive city, a shopper's paradise and northern lights.
Last stop,
Beautiful,
Landscape of massive mountains that envelop this place,
Orchids and vineyards give color to wine country.
Perhaps one day I will travel East,
Across the bridge of the town that birthed confederation,
Over Canada's ocean playground
Into the land of conservation parks and wild.
Alas,
A world of difference,
Weaves us together,
'Tis a spectacular northern land:
Canada.

Elia Viviani
Terrebonne, QB

Breezing with the Wind

Whirling and swirling are the ways of the light winds,
Who has ever taken time to understand them?
Lightly, it graces the body, gently delivering desirable coolness,
Nightly, across the horizon, making temperate its weather,
Have you ever thought, "What stirs up the waves in the oceans?"

If only I could hold you and find the source of your strength,
Shall I ask, the air masses circling south, clockwise and north,
counterclockwise?
Then, will the winds build cones, even larger and in taller cranes,
Powerfully, rising to the sky, with its branded hurricanes, from
the seas,
Landing where it chooses, wreaking havoc in its wake.

The wind velocity determines what it delivers to us,
Breeze, biting storms, cyclones or hurricanes.
I have heard it said twice, "Even the wind drives the rain,"
Thrice that, "the wind starts from the East,"
Fourthly, "the wind never shields its sword in the West."

As if it cares, the wind rises without a pillar in its frame,
Fetched, without an arm stretched from its mane,
Uproots, without a rake attached to its feet.
Rising high out of reach without a ladder for its climb.
It is fruitless grappling with the mighty wind,

The winds cloud all, on its ever present intent,
Who can hold it, when it chooses to blow?
Silent or whistling, soothing or crashing,
Like a smoke from a piper's chalice,
It blows and blows the air in its earthen vessel.

Wherever this wind blows, that is where I should go,
Who can blame me for not resisting you?

Cash Onadele
Dallas, TX

She Comes for Me

Here I lie in my darkest hour
Free of thought and any power
She comes to me
As the tears flow with no place left to go
She comes for me
When nothing more can go wrong and it's for true peace that I long
She comes for me
When shelter sought can nowhere be found
And my voice no longer carries sound
She comes for me
Oblivious of her intent
I do know though that she is not heaven-sent
She comes for me
Alone in a world where none comprehend
She says she'll be my true friend
She comes for me
I can only deny her advances for so long
She promises to right all the wrongs
She comes for me
Seductive as only a woman can be
I fear that I might go with her the next time
She comes for me

Erica Gallaread
Richmond, CA

Parental Advice

When the sun comes up in the morning
It signals the start of a new day
It's yours to use as you wish too
What will you do and what will you say

Will you use it for something worthwhile
That will brighten someone else's day
Or selfishly use it for self
Not caring what others might say

Each moment you're given is precious
Each second of every new day
I pray that you really won't waste it
That's what I'd tell you if I had the say

It's advice from one who has been there
For this isn't my very first day
So I as one who's a parent
Do implore you to hear what I say

But still it is yours for the choosing
Remember it's yours not my day
So don't listen to me, do what you want
And please say what you want to say

Dave Leiker
Hays, KS

We as parents can only give good advice, but in the end we still want our children to be independent and hope they learn from their mistakes.

The Heart

The heart is the inner self
that thinks, feels and decides
The heart has a much broader
meaning than it does to the modern mind
The heart is that which is
central to a person
The heart is the happiest
when it beats for others to help
and not when it beats for sins
The heart refers to some
aspect of human personality
all emotions are expressed by the heart
love and hate, joy and sorrow
peace and bitterness, courage and fear,
the thinking processes are
being carried by the heart
God knows our hearts
He knows us inside out!

Erlinda Roberts
Marshall, NC

What inspired me to write this poem? I know God inspired me to write it because he knew it would be published and a lot of people would read it —and some of them would be changed. My husband James, who is a veteran, said that I have good spiritual insight, and I think he is right! God is good! He created the body with complete parts; one of them is the heart which is central to a person. I love my creator. I believe in his Spirit that teaches, guides and directs us what to do!

His Last Name

I'd practice my vows in the mirror, as if
tomorrow was the day he'd lift my veil.
There wasn't a date marked on the
calendar yet, but only time would tell.
I didn't hint to my mother that he was my first,
but my father was convinced without the words.
He told me he'd give me his last name, but for
a girl at seventeen, being naive was my mistake.
From time to time, I'd picture the dress in my
head, along with the shoes I know I could've
never walked in. But the calendar must have
known there wouldn't be an event…
Your dress has been bought, and I bet it's beautiful,
but you can have his last name, because it's unusual.
My father's satisfied with him being engaged,
because he didn't want me to have his last name.
You've been practicing your vows in the mirror,
because tomorrow is your wedding day.
I never pictured you in the picture, but
by this time tomorrow, you'll have his last name.
He said he'd give me his last name, but he gave it to
you instead, and now, I'm just the girl who believed
the words Steven Searle said to me one night in a bed.

Shayla Mayhugh
Chickasha, OK

Dream World America

There was a chicken farmer from Ohio who dreamt of a sunken
   treasure off of the Florida coast.
His dream came true when he found gold and silver in a Spanish
   ship that
sunk in the Atlantic Ocean.
His Dream World America....
There was a coal miner's son who saw the Russian Sputnik orbit
   the Earth.
He then wanted to be a rocket scientist but his father wanted him
   to be a
coal miner.
He continued to work on small rockets and finally became a
   rocket scientist.
His Dream World America....
I didn't have any dreams, World.
My parents got me through the Depression of 1929.
I went to high school and spent three years in World War II,
   US Army.
I have the right to speak freely and right to vote.
I married a beautiful girl after the war and had a wonderful family.
I am now eighty-four years old.
"Wait a minute; this Dream World America is for everyone. I had
   my dream too and did not know it...."
God bless America, always....

Hayes Russell
Pittsburgh, PA

*I will be ninety-two years old in February, and I want to dedicate this poem, and
all the other writings I have done through the years, to my granddaughter Susan
Bauman. She types all my writings and corrects my spelling. I love you.*

Becoming Me

This is insane and hard to believe
This is crazy and not a joke to me
I don't believe it and never will
I refuse to stand so still
As the snow melts it's all ubiquitous
As the leaves fall it's not suspicious
Spring fades and it's gone forever
Summer comes for another never
Even since I could breathe
Even since I could understand
You make me believe that I'll never receive
Promises that belong to every man
I believe in me, and my voice
Something that is my choice
You say it's not my fault, that it's never meant to be
But how could I believe you when you won't even let me be me
I will be me and only me
Nothing that you are
I will be the best of me
A dream not too far
This is all I think about
It's all I know
I will make my own light
To make my path glow

Dakota J. McDaniel
Davisburg, MI

The Taste of Misery

So many words unspoken,
A gift of a wounded heart chosen,
Such a beautiful character defamed,
Heartfelt emotions gone in flames,
Happiness becomes one with confusion,
Compassionate memories forgotten,
Soul drifted away from this weary
Mortal body of mine beyond a vast distance,
Mind trembles with fear, a breakdown approaches near,
Life situation avoids the light stare,
No one left here to care,
Judgement attempts to compare,
Death seems to gently whisper,
Heart starts to quiver,
Hope loses its place,
Dark shadows become one fate,
Past repeats the same awkward mistakes,
A change much too late,
Hatred refrains from stalling,
Loneliness awakes its calling,
Life span severely shortened,
Eyes continue to be tormented,
Anger now a kin of me, enemies taken hold of me,
Trust with its pity befriended me,
Hurt establishes history,
Awakened by life dreadful misery!

Cory Simpson
Charleston, WV

The Room Upstairs

This room upstairs is happy
so much joy and light.
This room upstairs is happy,
baby takes first sight.

This room upstairs is sunny
she sits there to play.
This room upstairs is sunny,
never go away.

This room upstairs has books,
learning all the time.
This room upstairs has books
and did not show a sign.

This room upstairs now has curtains
no sun to be seen.
This room upstairs now has curtains,
kids can be so mean.

This room upstairs is dark,
no smile on her face.
This room upstairs is dark
in absence of embrace.

This room upstairs is empty.
It really isn't fair.
The room upstairs is empty,
leaving the family in despair.

Kelly Humphrey
Racine, OH

On a Clear Day: September 11, 2001

A clear blue sky all around, peace and comfort did abound
Being at their place of peace, not expecting it would cease

High up in the sky above, there was no brotherly love
Upon the buildings they were in, sparks and death were to begin

Astonishment to eyes as seen, who in this world could be so mean
Evacuating buildings high above, yelling, screaming, flying like
a dove

Belief was not there to see, everyone was trying to flee
Dust and ash came down from the sky; it covered the ground
and cars nearby

The people were running to find a safe place; to everyone this
was a total disgrace
Who in the world would ever have thought America could have
ever been sought

The planes were full of people like you and me, off to their
destinations wherever they may be,
Men of another country aboard, people crying for help dear Lord

They took the planes away from us to carry out their plans of
trust, no lives were
Valuable to them, and they were desperate, angry men

They didn't care the harm they caused and didn't care that lives
were lost
America free had no alarm that people like this would cause
such harm

Unbelievable that so much was lost at such a worthless,
priceless cost
We bow our heads and pray for peace and pray for those who
are deceased

For those who suffer in pain and sorrow, there will be a
brighter tomorrow

Betty Morgan
Mesa, AZ

It's Sad

It's sad that little kids have to die.
Parents are left here asking God why
There's no reply.
God knows he has full control.
I save them from all the misery that is in the earth daily.
He sees another sight that you can't see.
He says parents have no fear.
I am taking care of all things.
These kids are right here with me you will see.
It's sad that my own people talk behind my back.
It's sad that I am black and always getting attack.
It's sad that I only went to work.
Unfortunately I got seriously hurt.
I am grateful I am not buried under the dirt.
I am still here just a little hurt.
It's sad now I lost my first house.
My mother had to lose her spouse.
It's sad that cancer kills people daily.
Just thankful for Jesus dying on the tree,
For everyone to be set free from all sins.
And one day we will join his family,
Up there in the heavenly gates,
To have no more pain or sorrows.
For we all will be blessed with another tomorrow.
It's sad that life has so many ups and downs,
But I know Jesus can heal all our frowns,
When we go to Heaven and receive our crowns.

Katina Newton
Washington, DC

Song of Mourning

Life is fleeting,
Ephemeral,
And sweet…
'Tis the story of two souls who meet…
Joyous,
The days unforgotten…
Blessed,
Your paths did cross…
Even after passing,
Do not mourn for the ones you've lost…
They rest in eternal slumber,
With God their soul resides…
Rejoice,
They went to Heaven,
And live eternal life…
Hello…
Goodbye…
And hello…
'Twas your heart that touched upon my soul…

Robert Roman
Northridge, CA

Tainted Love

Tainted love so bitter,
Was once all aglitter.
But he stepped out and cheated.
Thus, she felt mistreated.
Divorce was the only course.
Her ire became a force.
So strong it threatened to drown,
All who were around.
The end came.
It was a shame.
Because once upon a time,
Their love had been divine.
Their lives had been entwined.
A stronger love you could not find.
But he had to cheat,
Thus, tainting their love.

Darlene Thomson
Newport, RI

Bilingual Johnny

I was born in Mexicali
But my folks were born right here
I was taught down in the valley
Still bilingual every year
My OB garden was my wish
Where a girl asked by the pier
Do you speak English or Spanish?
"I'm bilingual still my dear"
Budweiser or Corona
Which one is your favorite beer?
Everybody says "cerveza"
That's the language that I hear
I still look a bit Caucasian
When I'm staring at a mirror
I'm that John that looks at that Juan
So let's get this language clear
Hey these two have to be amigos
Got dual-citizenship for the cheer
We're the same from our head to our toes
With an equal ability fear
California towns are in Spanish
We keep Mexican food in gear
And make great tacos with your fish
'Cause equality's getting near
Every day, I prey, 'cause we're
Still bilingual with a tear

Juan R. Nogales
Calexico, CA

Hello again, it's me "dog." Any day Calexico will be hit with another earthquake, worse, and things and people will break. So together, if something's wrong, we've got to fix it. Don't hide your money, donate, 'cause many are not as fortunate as you. The only war we all have in common is cancer. It just got into my father's blood. God please give my father more years, he's the kind of person you wanted. If you want to hear me sing, come Saturday mornings in November to Calexico's "Farmers Market" at Crummett Park. Mom, Dad and Tasha, I love you forever.

Realization

In teary eyes I see realization
Sad from mistakes and hesitation
Life is patience
But patience to be a morgue patient
Depression's power devours
But life's lessons are depression with every hour
It's always too late when you realize
When you can finally see your real eyes
Is time wasted when it's fate you're chasing?
Is it you or me in the mirror of realization?

Mike McCluskey
Holly, MI

Mike McCluskey is a true testament to the art of poetry, continuing to write in vain within a world that chooses to ignore true art with heart. Edgar Allan Poe is rolling over in his grave appalled at how the world has disrespected the dedicated, creative, thought provoking artists of our time with ignorance and blindness. Mike McCluskey is the author of thirty-two self-published books including: nine full-length poem books, fourteen poetry chapbooks and twenty-five short stories. For ordering information refer to facebook.com/dark man inc. and the bookstore at BLURB.com.

On My 25ᵗʰ Birthday

One score and five I celebrate,
my youthful visions seem like nets
cast out in turmoiled seas; now they're
torn patchwork things, sewn with regrets.

Knowledge, old phantom I have sought,
and Beauty's subtle form to trace,
(while sorrow all unbidden came
and carved with tears a wiser face).

Old dreams are past. New ones arise
with deeper roots. Yet still would I
hitchhike on rockets to the moon,
toss snowflakes back into the sky.

Within these searching, curious years
my universe all richly lies,
come blow the candles out like stars
and bid new constellations rise!

Helen Yale
Pleasant Hill, CA

Families Are Like Fruit Salad

Some are as sweet as peaches
and some are just sour grapes.

Then you have your tart cherries
and your juicy oranges.

There are always a few crisp apples
and mushy bananas.

Throw in a few nuts and marshmallows
with a little tangy pineapple.

There you have the makings
of a nice fruit salad.

But the one thing that holds it all
together is the dressing, *and that's the mother.*

Helen M. Burgess
Lawrenceburg, KY

Untitled

Someday you'll be grown and on your own, but we will be here
   and always near.
So when things get you down, don't be afraid to come around.
You are bright, kind, talented, and have the world at your feet.
So keep going forward and don't let yourself be beat.
You are capable of so much, so let us be your crutch.
Wherever you need us to boost you up, come home and we will fill
   your cup.
And when we aren't able, we will help you be capable.
And later, when you marry and have your children, you will
   understand that they are one in quadrillion.
Then when we have passed our time, you will continue and be fine.
Your husband and children will then be there to fill your cup
   again, and bring you happiness without end.
And when all is said and done, you have made us prouder than no
   other one.
So continue to enjoy and love your life, no matter the
   occasional strife.
In the end you will see, your children are what will make you free.
Believe in and cherish them like no others,
because nothing compares to being fathers and mothers.

Kelly Kremposky
Slatington, PA

The inspiration for this poem is my daughter Lizzy. She makes us proud everyday!

Whispers

I hear a sound of softness,
A smell of sweet perfume,
A voice so meek, meek subdue.
Flowers and sunshine, as in the month of June.
A smile towards you, one for me,
A mouthed hello, a whispered hi!
Feeling all chummy, and anew.
I glance to the left, then the right.
People are talking, my eyes start to wander,
I am looking around the room.
It's messing with my mind.
People keep talking; people keep whispering.
I feel a sense of panic,
What are they trying to say?
The softness is now pounding, the smell not so sweet.
My flowers are dying,
My smile now a frown, head looking down.
Want to say goodbye, feel like crying.
Whispers louder than words.
Whispers now in my head.
Whispers not so meek.
Whispers once so soft, now overwhelming.
Inner paranoia.
How quickly it's all turned.
Sweet softness, self-destruction, I have to go,
Inner defeat.

Tavita Edwards
Gridley, CA

Where There Is Hope

But she was just a woman
and he only a man.
And neither was prepared
for life's merciless demand.

Every penny was needed,
for bills had to be paid.
They worked throughout the weeks,
gave nearly all that was made.

The little that they did save
was used for food and gas.
And the gathered loose change
was offered at Sunday's mass.

But the earth did yet still turn,
bringing blissful seasons.
The wondrous joy of spring
filled hearts with hope and reasons.

With crisp air and sunlit skies,
their courage did revive.
They loved one another.
With pure faith they did survive.
Just a man and a woman,
grateful to be alive.

Rachel Sehn
Somerset, PA

My Season

Spring, the time of new beginnings;
Spring, are you coming this year?
Spring, the trees need you here…
Spring, the birds are singing;
Spring, please hurry here!

Spring always comes;
Spring, do not be late.
Spring is my favorite time of year…
Spring, bring pretty flowers;
Spring, bring slow showers.

Spring is no doubt late;
Spring was buried in snow…
Spring may be just a little slow.
Spring… spring… spring…
Spring, please bring extra love this year!

Bettye M. Butler
Oxford, MS

Too Late

It happens as we tarry here
with our petty fights,
our minor plights.

Despair consumes a hopeless heart,
souls ascend to Heaven's gates,
a hand reaches out—where none awaits.

Convenient blindness to other's despair,
a deaf ear to a child's cry,
while deliverance stands idly by.

Fearful of compassionate involvement,
afraid to face the dying's fate,
we stand and watch till... too late. Too late.

Kathi Foy
Yucca Valley, CA

I Have a Dream

"I am happy to join with you today in what will go down
In history as the greatest demonstration for freedom in
The history of my nation." *Martin Luther King Jr.* had a
Dream of freedom, that black and white were one.
I am here to better his dream, to live on what died in
1963. I will die a legend, because I too have a dream.
Many have lowered my self-esteem. Yet I strive to the
Extreme. I will excel, even when going through hell.
Media has given the Negro people a bad check, a check
Which has come back marked "insufficient funds."
Martin Luther King Jr., I will not let you down for my
Dream is way too big for it to be just a dream
As a *black* woman I will represent. I too have a dream.
I dream of becoming a clinical psychologist, helping
The ones in need of attention, holding out my hand…
Extension.
I dream of having my reality be better than just the
Words I have spoken today. I will not delay for this
Dream is more than just a dream. This dream is my only
Chance to gain my victory. This is the time to prove
To everyone who doubted me. I have a dream of success
With that, let freedom ring!
Now is the time to make justice a reality.
I too have a dream Martin Luther King.

Moriah Cooper
Grovetown, GA

*In this poem there are parts from Martin Luther King Jr.'s "I Have a Dream"
speech to show how the world then is no different than the world now.*

A Baby Comes

When a baby comes…
it is not empty handed,
not naked,
not alone.

When a baby comes…
it brings in its tiny hands:
a world filled with love,
clothed in a gown of miraculous beauty
and wrapped in a delicate blanket of dreams.

When a baby comes…
it fulfills your desires
and takes your heart away.

A baby comes…
Not empty handed.
Not naked.
Not alone.

Tonia Heifner
Marianna, FL

I was inspired in 2015 by Eyvie. Each birth brings a new world and each takes a part of my heart. This is dedicated with love to my daughters Rebecca and Jennifer, grandchildren Joncy, Annastasia, Joseph, Nicholas, Liberty, Christian, and Justice, and my first great-grandchild Eyvie.

Mom's Journey to Heaven

Although your time on earth is done
Your journey to Heaven has just begun.
As the Lord commands with one loud yell
Your soul shall descend from your body so frail.
As you walk through Heaven's door
You will be greeted by loved ones who've gone on before.
As you walk and talk with them there
Could you let them know we still care and miss them so?
And when you behold the glory of God's face so sweet
I know you will bow down and kneel at his feet.
He will take you by the hand and say, "Arise my precious daughter,"
And you will abide in his presence with awe and wonder.
And after you kiss and hug him so tight
Could you remind him of us down here that's going to be
    struggling tonight?
We know you're in a much better place
But that doesn't stop the tears from rolling down our face.
I know what you would say if you were still here:
There's nothing wrong with a few little tears.
If crying is something you must do, then cry if you must
But remember this too,
I'm never really far away all you must do is kneel down and pray.
And when you speak a kind word or two, that's me speaking
    through you.
So dry your eyes and put on a smile, I'll see you in just a while.
As we shed one last tear it's because we will truly miss you here.
In all this world so grand and true there will never be another to
    take the place of our dear mother.

Margie Pierson
Milford, DE

Pitter-Patter Pitter-Patter

For Rose—when Molly chased Cody around the house or went
out for a walk, those soft fuzzy four paws sang:
Pitter-patter
Pitter-patter

For Rose—Molly waited so patiently in the car, when Richard and
you went out for dinner. The joy she had jumping up and down
when you returned. Those soft fuzzy four paws sang:
Pitter-patter
Pitter-patter

For Rose—January 3rd, 2005. The pitter-patter was silenced, for
those soft fuzzy four paws sang no more. The good Lord decided
to take Julie to Heaven and took Molly to keep her company.

For Rose—the roll and crackling of thunder during a storm is not
what I hear. It is Julie, throwing and rolling the ball for Molly's
playtime, the drumming of the rain on the roof is not what we think.
It is Molly chasing the ball and those soft fuzzy four paws singing—
Pitter-patter
Pitter-patter

Steve Schumm
Bloomingburg, NY

*My friend Rose called me in January of 2005 to tell me that her dog Molly had
passed, could I write a poem? Later that week, Rose informed me that her relative
Julie had passed. She believed that the Lord called Molly from this life to keep
Julie company in Heaven. Then I knew I could write "Pitter-Patter Pitter-Patter."*

My Dream!

I dreamt last night of flying
Soaring high over buildings
As I maneuver under cables
Careful, not to get my wings entangled.

Soaring among the clouds,
Over mountains and lakes,
Meadows, colored like rainbows,
Breathing the fragrance to fill my broken heart.

I see a demon with long crooked teeth,
And talons razor sharp
Hiding between shadows waiting for his prey.

I fly towards him to save that screaming soul.
I'm falling, falling hard. As I hit the pavement,

The demon approaches dripping blood,
Blood. From his fangs.
A foul stench begins to surround me.

Desperately, I flap my wings
To get back to the sky
To safety I flap, flap, flap.

He's gaining on me
Must get away from him.
Talons, ripping at my legs,
Out of breath I soar to the sky
To safety and out of this dream.

Anna Kowsky
Palm Desert, CA

Autumn's Deadly Dance

Her name is Autumn: an exquisite and striking beauty with only three months to live. Her skin is pale flawlessness, gently glowing behind her faintly steaming breath. Her hair is a slow fire, dry crimsons and auburns caressing deep chestnuts and cinnamons as she thoughtlessly spins in a sleepy dance.

Her name is Autumn. She is the forsaken queen of cornstalks and jack-o'-lanterns, all sharing in her morbid grace. She is the mother of cold winds and barren trees. Though the freshest of sweet ciders come to flow in abundance during her reign, few goblets within her inconvenienced dominion are ever raised in celebration of her unusual gifts.

Her name is Autumn. Upon each frost-laden morning, she feasts on single bites of sunlight and quickly digests the verdant gifts of her older sister. And waiting within her final mouthful, beneath the waning harvest moon, lies the poison of her promised demise.

Her name is Autumn, and we should bow in honor of her brief and deadly dance… for she only has three months to live…

Richard F. Keene Jr.
North Smithfield, RI

Horrid Skin

You tell me I'm stupid because of my tattoos
I tell you you're wrong
My skin is what's stupid
I'm covered in scars from days where I thought
A rope could solve my problems
I'm covered in self hate
Self-destruction
Everlasting disgusted
I've lived a life where pain was the awakening
From my beautiful imaginary world
Time flew by as I sat and stared
At the blank wall of my ruined mind
My heart drenched in
Pain
Sorrow
And agony
Of the people I used to know
I saw my life being ripped and torn little by little
Diseases dripping from every bone in my body
My skin is the reminder
Of all the pent up aggression and rage of who I was
So now
I've covered my skin in ink
So I finally see a piece of art on a wrecked canvas

Anna Lalumondier
Shawnee, KS

Icarus

The fate of Icarus, a story to be told,
A lesson for those who think themselves bold.
Prisoners, father and son, kept across the sea
Sought to escape, to once again be free.
"Let us fly away with wings of wax and feathers.
Let us hope for fair winds and weather."

The day arrived and off the prisoners flew.
Yet the tragedy waiting, no one knew.
The father cautioned, "Do not fly toward the sun
For the wax wings will melt—the wings come undone."
The ecstasy of soaring aloft, the youth threw caution aside;
His father's warnings, he forgot and denied.

Icarus flew up higher and higher
With his own impending doom nigher and nigher
All at once, his wings came apart
Which caused great pain to his father's heart.
He retrieved his son from the sea below
And carried him home with spirit low.

The lesson here is truly for one and all—
Heed the wise lest you too shall fall.
Know your limits; do not let pride carry away.
If Icarus had done so, he would have lived another day.

Dominic Figueroa
Napa, CA

I have grown up in the Bay Area in California. I began to take an interest in poetry in middle school. I wrote my first poem as I looked upon the beautiful mountains of the Napa Valley. The greatest achievement of my life was opening my heart to experience authentic goodness, truth, and beauty.

Grief

Raindrops slide down windowpanes
Like tears that slowly fall
But from my eyes that watch them
No teardrops fall at all.
How fortunate the grey clouds that cry
With no regrets or fears.
How terrible to live with grief
That is too deep for tears.

Millie Heister
Kalispell, MT

Right Time and Place

The leaves of tables spread
All are gathered dead
To peer before them at each other
Peer around… through one another
Never knowing, caring, hoping,
Outside in with fork and spoon
Not too late but not too soon
Not too much but say enough
Ambition's never sterner stuff
And bugs will eat the table leaves
Spread for the gathered dead

Robert Aukerman
Centennial, CO

Untitled

Obligated to stand tall and firm
When in reality I wish to grovel at your feet
Beg of you to be mine once more
Dazzle me once again with your wonder and glory
Provide me once more with the joy and fire
That your company provides
Two individuals come together with no pretense
Expecting nothing more
Than to be and let be
To live and in time to love...
Recollections cradled in my mind for warmth
A desperate coveting to return
With the searing realization I cannot
My subconscious cries out for you
In moments of complacency
Drawn to a time when every instant was you
And each moment energetic and complete
It seems nearly sadistic
For life to provide such an awe inspiring gift
Only to have it ripped away...
Or perhaps I am merely a masochist
For searching out the stability of love
In a creation as unpredictable
As the human heart

Brett Nathan Humphreys
San Francisco, CA

Time Machine

Miles and minutes keep flying by
Still figuring out the how and the why
Dozens of strangers I see every day
Passing some time before passing away
Riding this blue ball year after year
Spinning in space like a magnetic gear
Thousands are joining thousands will leave
Under the power of this time machine
Living for pleasure or treasure each day
Don't understand there's a price to be paid
Establishing names one day no one recalls
The strength and the plans one day spoiled
So much in this life—not quite as it appears
Men boast control, but are bound by their fears
Spend their days gathering then leave it behind
We really have nothing but time

Fred Plant
Saugerties, NY

My Friends and I Ride

Quiet… can you hear it
Lub, lub, lub, lub, lub…
Here they come: old, young and in between
All kinds of bikes, all sizes of riders, women and men together

Straddling their machines, helmets in place, headlights on
Each looking out for one another
No man/woman left behind no bike left alone

The goal is to make life better for an underprivileged group
Funds raised, supplies bought and delivered
School supplies, fans for the elderly—if someone knows a need let
them know
And we will plan how we will go about helping someone's need
get met

By just looking at our group you may think we would not be
trustworthy,
But when we ride up and give the donated items or cash, the tears
will flow at this honorable deed

From all walks of life, white collar, blue collar and retirees all
pull together
Hoping you will see past their tattoos, bandanas and boots

My friends and I ride—what do you do?

Pamela Griffin
Rockingham, NC

Sweet Penny

Sweet Penny died. They say the good die young.
Sweet Penny wasn't young, but she was good.
She never complained even when she felt ignored.
All she had to do was make a noise and doors opened.

She was a wonderful addition to the family.
She had a family that loved her.
She was a follower not a leader.
She never lost her cool and paid attention to details.

She was a friend to all, especially the youngsters.
They had so many questions about her.
The biggest was how old she was.
She never said.

She had many stories whispered about her.
She lost her good buddy in Key Largo.
She never said how much it hurt.
We never brought it up.

She was content to sit around and watch TV.
She loved her back rubs. It was a nightly tradition.
She slept a lot and she ate a lot.
We respected that.

Did I say she was a wonderful addition to the family?
Did I say she had a family that loved her?
I did. But I didn't say my final most important thing.
Sweet Penny, sweet dreams and good night.

Arlene Saltzman
Miami, FL

You Can Do Anything

You can do anything
You can do anything

Anything you can do, I can do

You can do anything
You can do anything

I don't do anything

You can do anything
You can do anything

I don't do anything that you can do

Joy V. Everett
Alvin, TX

K. A. J. E.

We are the perfect couple,
We're just not in the perfect situation,
Distance has always been trouble,
But with you, I'm looking to make it amazing

No matter how far you are,
No matter the miles between us,
I know that we are apart,
But the distance won't defeat us

Nothing can really separate
Two hearts that really care,
I know you can't feel me right now,
But I'm holding your hand, I'm always there
I'm always here, physically, emotionally, and spiritually,
Though you can't hear me
I send you my vibes hoping that you're feeling me

I know distance is scary,
But have faith my dear, it'll make a turn for the best
Distance is only temporary,
For I am working towards success
And you, my princess,
My future, you are my success

Adrian Aguilar
Snyder, TX

Missing someone gets easier everyday because even though you are one day further from the last time you saw them, you are one day closer to the next time you will. Distance is but space and numbers, it is only temporary and means so little when someone means so much. True dedication: A. M. A. A. K. A. J. E.

My Secret Crush

Graced by her presence, doing my best
to stay in the presence of mind
When she's near my mind tends
to veer towards a default network
Trapped in muse, getting an eyeful
of her pulchritude, observing every detail
I try not to ogle too much,
my heart has a hint of agog
My agog doesn't lie in a bucket
of lust and how she is in bed
I don't think of her as just some
sexy woman that I deem worthy
I've noticed her pulchritude runs deep,
she's marvelous trapped in a margin
The space around the margin,
I see is frabjous in a seventy-two font
The inquiring thoughts of what
it would be like if I had a chance
I can't download this emotion because
we don't have a wifi connection
I want her to know who I am,
the only thing is that she's unavailable
With thought of her only being
or loving me sometimes saddens me
I can't get my hopes up, sometimes
I can be a sucker for something I've never had
I'm just a noun composing adjectives
with adverbs trying to modify my verbs
Every time I see her I do my best
to keep my composure
Various thoughts of her linger about,
I'd rather keep my feelings a secret
An anonymous admirer that sees beauty
in everything while thinking about the possibilities

Lonnie Jones Jr.
Lake Charles, LA

What Makes a Lifetime?

You often hear people say, "That was a lifetime ago"
How long is that and how are we supposed to know?
A lifetime is more than a number of years in succession
Growing older they move more rapidly in progression
A lifetime is made up of so many hellos and good byes
A journey filled with the lowest lows and highest highs
One day there will come that final closing of your eyes
Only then will you learn if there is an afterlife as a prize
So live each day and enjoy each moment and every hour
Let your light shine as if a beacon from high in a tower
For if one lifetime is all that each is given
We should for this one be ultimately driven
To seek the joys of sunny todays and bright tomorrows
Yet endure cold penetrating rains filled with sorrows
For in the end your lifetime will be defined
By a large number of hellos and of acts so kind

Sally Jackson
Metairie, LA

Snow White, It's Spring!

Delighted creatures, reunited, leapt
in dance as sparrows flew with whirring sound.
A bluebird strutted, chirped a thought — profound!
All quiet blooming trees, (each secret kept),
then rustled yellow limbs, aroused who slept.
Snow White's romance had blossomed near this ground.
Her amber hair once swirled here, flower-crowned:
received by magic dwarfs, who smiled and wept,
this gentle child created trilling song.
Vibrations thrilled these woods, enchanted place!
When kissed, she moves! Alive! And chipmunks fling
themselves and form a busy circled throng.
A comet streaks from vacant outer space.
It whirls itself into our maiden's ring.
Her gallant prince is standing now. His strong,
yet timid, hands each lift her bridal lace.
Ignited sigh, in fantasy, is Spring!

Joyce Elaine Wheeler
Long Beach, CA

Trees Dancing

The trees danced as old man winter blew his tune.
They rejoiced in the promised return of youthful summer in June.

The fall, like Adam and Eve, stripped them naked in the cold
and rain,
But, promised to be beyond Solomon's splendor in the spring.

That's how it is with God and His care.
For the believer there is much to share.

When the chill and cold of trouble blow,
Remember that Jesus said He must go

To prepare a place for believers to dwell
But, for those who reject that place is Hell.

So we dance before a dark world so bare,
But we remember that we have "good news" to share.

Just as the trees dance in the winter wind for the promise of June,
We as Christians dance for Jesus who will return soon.

The promise He has made is as sure as the seasons,
But He delays for many reasons.

Amidst the tribulation and trouble that come our way,
Remember Jesus said He would return on "that day."

Do not give up hope or refuse to believe,
Just remember He's coming when you see the leaves.

Bobby E. Hopper
Linden, AL

One Alone

One alone
Lonely as a desert breeze
I may wander where I please all alone
Yet I keep longing just to rest awhile all alone
Still thinking about where my sweetheart's tender eyes are
Hoping for them to take the place of the sand and skies
All the world forgotten in this woman's smile
One alone to be my own
I alone to know her caresses and await for only her
The one with whom I will spend eternity
At her call I will give her my all
All my life I have wandered alone to find this one true love
This would be a magic world if she were mine alone
I alone long to be with her all alone forever
And as long as she's mine alone I will never be anymore
It's because of her my path alone has been our journey
That journey has lasted together for over forty-three years
That journey of love has given us three great boys
And three of the greatest grandkids
They all have made us very proud
Now that's a journey to remember
Alone no more, I thank them all for the journey of joy

Larry N. Daley
Wappingers Falls, NY

*"One Alone" is a poem started by my father who was dating my mother in 1949
and 1950, two years before I was born. I found the rough writings after his death
in 1975. Poetry seems to run in our blood: my father Lawrence Daley Sr., myself
Lawrence Daley Jr., my son Lawrence Neal Daley III and both of his kids, my
grandson Sean Lawrence Daley, and my two granddaughters Megan Lynn Daley
and Deanna Celeste Daley. The special thing about "One Alone" is the first thirteen
and a half lines were written from my father to my mother. The bottom half I wrote
to my wife, kids, and grandkids. They all have filled my life with love and joy.
My wife has given me a journey to remember and because of her I will never be
one alone. Lawrence Neal Daley Sr. died in 1975 at age 49 September 16th; two
of his kids were born on that date (Dr. Edwin Daley and my sister Lanette Daley
Siford). My mother died at age 47 but they didn't stay one alone; they continued
with many new branches of the family tree with seven kids in her short life.*

Index of Poets

A

Aguilar, Adrian 312
Akhtar, Eman 157
Alcayaga, Aniceta P. 87
Allen, Patricia A. 153
Anderson, Dillen 188
Angle, Ruth 186
Arroyo, Yvonne B. 147
Aukerman, Robert 306
Austin, Patricia 226

B

Bangs, Gregory 65
Baranyk-Smith, Elijah 225
Bastian, Roxanne Patrice 133
Bauer, Sharon R. 106
Belisle, Julie 142
Bennett, Samuel 6
Bleich, Jennifer 227
Blessing, Leonard 20
Boone, Virginia L. 262
Bostick, Ky 204
Brabant, Ruth 196
Brace, Hannah 149
Brattland, Marian W. 62
Brewer, Carol D. 98
Broomes, Lloyd 7
Brown, Cleo E. 101
Bruno, Theresa 185
Burgess, Helen M. 292
Butler, Bettye M. 296

C

Cambilargiu, Joh 259
Carr, Lisa 102
Caruso, Mary Ann 209
Chevraux, Thomas 260

Childson, Shelli Anne 191
Chilson, Sydney 31
Chowdhury, Seema 136
Christensen, Sarah Danielle 211
Christie-Brooks, Patricia E. 105
Clanton, Teresa 9
Clark, Alice M. 54
Clough, Roger M. 161
Cody, Erasala B. 170
Coldwell, Morgan Elizabeth 42
Cole, Yvonne E. 224
Collins, Kay Jo 125
Conroy, Amber 172
Cook, David 34
Cooper, Moriah 298
Correa, Ellen J. 49
Courtepatte, Tara-Lynn 148
Cox, Nancy L. 96
Croly, Anne 236
Cronin, Lizzi M. 258
Cronk, Kathleen 173
Cuellar, Anabel 169
Cull, Bev 158
Cunningham, Beverley A. 30

D

Daley, Larry N. 317
Daley, Marlene 273
Davidson, Kayla 214
Davis, Diana L. 97
Delice, Fritz-Gerald 43
De Loof, Rebecca 86
Demicco, Joseph P. 27
Denney, Sharon A. 80
Deslauriers, JoAnne 81
Dinkins, Timothy 132
Downing, Wilda 189
Drost, Victoria 19
Drown, Paula C. 254
Duckery, Nicole Rochelle 95

Duncker, William 171
Dunlap, Brandi 139
Dunlap, Donald D., Sr. 33

E

Earl, Frances 176
Edwards, Jodi-Kay 227
Edwards, Tavita 294
Eiland, Connie 123
Eldred, Donald R. 121
Elmquist, Linda 66
Emery, Janet L. 217
Engle, Whitney 228
Epstein, David 199
Esperanza, Gloria 68
Everett, Joy V. 311
Eye, Elisabeth 112

F

Faschingbauer, Loraine 104
Feezor, Wilmetta 240
Fierman, Regina 170
Figueroa, Dominic 305
Finley Foreman, Martha 32
Flores, Eduardo 162
Forte, Dan 141
Foy, Kathi 297
Frankland, Colleen N. 24
Franklin, Janine 207
Freeman, Jerry T. 83
Frost, Mollie 239

G

Gallaread, Erica 277
Gallimore, Connie 216
Gass, Alyssa 248
George, Charlotte 247
Gerace, Lauri J. 3
Gerlach, Jill D. 178
Godinho, Larry 218
Goldson, Barbara 78

Gough, Carol 4
Graber, Sandi 48
Green, Marie 28
Greenmun, Anna Louise 72
Gregg, Judy M. 46
Griffin, Pamela 309
Grimm, Sherry 255
Grochowski, Deborah 41
Gruettner, Joanne G. 182
Guefen, Lili 206

H

Hackett, Esther 57
Hagwood, Earline 29
Hamm, Marjorie 25
Hampton, Diane Loretta King 22
Hardcastle, Jackie 51
Harmison, Shirley 28
Hattendorf, Cecilia 267
Hawkins, Stephen M. 274
Hayden, Jo Ann M. 234
Heifner, Tonia 299
Heineman, Carol M. 93
Heister, Millie 306
Hellman-Lohr, Aisha 79
Henriquez, Sarah 183
Henry, Virginia 8
Hernandez, Denise 36
Hines, Carolyn 70
Hinkle, Kenneth 117
Hitz, Billy 253
Hitzemann, Marvin 241
Hoefert, Yvonne K. 116
Holladay, JaNeli 118
Hooks, Bernice 59
Hopper, Bobby E. 316
Houser, Gladys L. 146
Hull, Janice Richardson 143
Humphrey, Kelly 284
Humphreys, Brett Nathan 307
Hyatt, Ruby V. 85

I

Ingraham, Bridget 258

J

Jackson, Deb 229
Jackson, Sally 314
Jacobson, Sandra 150
Jakiel, Amber 174
Jennings, Geraldine 63
Jerden, Brian W. 266
Jett, Jonita 252
Jogan, Laurie 103
Johnson, Jack 251
Johnstone, Timothy H. 135
Jones, Ferris 219
Jones, Lonnie, Jr. 313
Joppie, Cleo 210
Jurado, Gabriella 220

K

Karson, Racquel Antoinette 159
Kash, Peggy J. 23
Keehn, Norm 38
Keene, Richard F., Jr. 303
Kempf, Joseph H. 10
Kern, Ronald C. 152
King, Veronica 197
Kissman, Dorothy E. 127
Klein, Howard C. 203
Knox, Tiffany 69
Kowsky, Anna 302
Kremposky, Kelly 293
Kuzmich, Anna 265

L

Lalumondier, Anna 304
Lauzon, Nancy 156
Lee, Tracey Travis 124
Legiec, Rachel 166
Leiker, Dave 278

Lieber, Linda J. 194
Lloyd, Tanner 268
Locke, Bonnie S. 163
Loeterman, Matthew 187
Long, Vera 205
Lorentz, Kathy 244
Lory, Robert C. 263
Lowery, Nicole 212
Lyn, Corey 175

M

MacHose Steiner, Carolyn 202
Mack, Lynette 179
Magaña Magaña, Kelli 239
Magill, Robert C. 129
Mahoney, Barbara A. 13
Maldonado, Gloria Rosas 111
Malin, Eleanor 71
Malinskaya, Marina 237
Mann, Hannah 167
Mannstedt, Thomas 213
Marsh, Judith 257
Mascia, Nanci 272
Mayhugh, Shayla 280
Mayou, James W. 50
McCluskey, Mike 290
McDaniel, Dakota J. 282
McDonald, Claire 94
McFadden, Irene 58
McFarlane, Dorothy Ann 221
McKillip, Judith M. 11
McLaughlin, Charlotte C. 233
Mellett, Susannah 12
Melvin, Lawrence 110
Merryman, Cierra 201
Michalowski, Jeffrey J. 56
Moon, Judy Pannell 200
Moore, Michael Gordon 235
Moran, Rhonda L. 161
Morgan, Betty 285
Morris, Bobbie 75
Moyer, Tim 2
Murray, Reginald W. 90

N

Nagel, Caroljo 155
Neagu, George V. 238
Neel, Saisa 180
Newton, Katina 286
Nickey, Amanda M. 269
Nieves, Celia 245
Noga, Ruth C. 74
Nogales, Juan R. 289
Nokes, Janice 16

O

Oberman, Lori 92
Odneal, Stephen Kent 209
Olli, Janice 114
Olmstead, Jeanette 243
Onadele, Cash 276
O'Rear, Christine 261
Osborne, Mary S. 100
O'Scannell, Molly 270
Owen, Heather Mairn 91

P

Pardo, Paula 37
Patterson, Andre 82
Paulsen, Laura L. 131
Payne, Deanna L. 271
Penwell, Katie 145
Perez, Lisa Marie 137
Peters, Samantha 154
Pierson, Margie 300
Plant, Fred 308
Plumbly, Judd 223
Plymale, Laurie 230

Q

Quarshie, Theresa L. 232

R

Ravikumar, Samyuktha 108
Rembert, David H., Jr. 166
Rice, Jennifer 1
Richardson, Diana 104
Richardson, Tommie 190
Riddick, Florence 120
Riddle, Frances 65
Ritzen, Janina Kylie 264
Roach, Rebecca 193
Roberson, Millette 115
Roberts, Erlinda 279
Roberts, Hannah N. 231
Robertson, Karli 242
Roman, Robert 287
Roper, Jewell 84
Roth, Diana 52
Russell, Hayes 281
Rutledge, Sharon G. 47

S

Salazar, Mollie G. 144
Saltzman, Arlene 310
Sanderson, Pat 44
Santiago, Louis R. 64
Schmitt, Lori 256
Schroll, Larry L. 134
Schumm, Steve 301
Sehn, Rachel 295
Selby, Barbara E. 107
Sharpe, Dianna 215
Sheridan, Ann 198
Shields, Doris 61
Shiller, Beth 21
Shugars, Caryl Van Alstyne 126
Simmons, Hermelinda 192
Simpson, April 39
Simpson, Cory 283
Smith, Roy A. 88
Smith-Cameron, Cecelia 222
Sorrell, Allison 99
Spears, Helen Margaret 26
Staley, Betty J. 122
Stickley, Jolly P. 55

Stradley, Robin N. 15
Strinden, Jerry 184
Strom, Lillian 77
Suchorski, Janet 250

T

Tellez, Leslie 184
Terry, Ron 164
Thayer, Jessica 89
Thieme, Donald A. 60
Thomson, Darlene 288
Thornton, Gary 208
Thorud, Ruth 119
Tobin, Mike 5
Torres, Jacquelyn R. 246
Townsend, J. Lillie 19
Tripodi, Tony 140
Trombley, Joan 130
Troxel-Spence, Virginia Diane 17
Tuayev, Kazbek M. 113
Tull, Mary Jean 259

V

Valente, Barbara J. 138
Vernon, Peta-Gaye 181
Viviani, Elia 275
Volpe, Rene 73

W

Walker-Boone, Jeri D. 35
Wallace, Danielle J. 168
Weber, Leo 67
Werner, Aleksandra 195
Wheeler, Joyce Elaine 315
White, Valerie L. 45
Williams, Jane 76
Wiseman, Tera Levette 18
Wolfe, Erna 109
Wood, Burnell Burns L. 160
Wooten, Aron 128

Y

Yale, Helen 291
Yarek, Cheryl 40
Yeck, Joan Patterson 165
Young, Guy B. 151
Young-Lionshows, Alice Marie 14
Yousse, Loraine 249
Yuzuki, Elaine J. 53

Z

Zweig, Theresa 177